# YEAR
## OF THE
# FIGHTER

## LESSONS FROM MY MIDLIFE CRISIS ADVENTURE

## Matt Deaton, Ph.D.

# Year of the Fighter:

## Lessons from my Midlife Crisis Adventure

ISBN 978-0-9892542-5-0

Edited by Deborah Stansil

Cover Photo by Matt Hamilton

Published by Notaed Press

# Contents

# Part V: The Lessons

# Chapter 1

# The Bloodsport Moment

June 18, 2016 – Dalton, Georgia

Behind the crowd near the steps into the ring, Matt on my left and Scott to my right, I started bobbing, then bouncing, then jumping.

Matt was worried the adrenaline dump would burn me out.

"Calm down... *calm down.*"

But the predator atmosphere had infected me. This guy wanted to kick my face like Mario had, except without Mario's remorse.

When the bell rang Logan Steele's abs lived up to his name – my kicks to his gut were having little effect.

He had better stamina than both of the boxers I'd fought, and seemed to really know what he was doing for a kickboxer with an 0-0 record.

And the kid could punch hard. *Real* hard.

He landed a string of solid headshots in rounds one and two that left me woozy. And mixing kicks into the exchange was proving exhausting. Despite months of training, I was at my physical limit.

Then at the beginning of the third round came an attack I'd never faced: a "Superman" punch.

Logan reared back as if he was going to throw a roundhouse kick to my thigh, but instead lunged forward like the man of steel flying into Zod, transferring all his power through his knuckles, into my jaw.

I was rocked like never before. In a daze, a voice came to me:

> *"Oh man, I'm about to get knocked out... But maybe that's a good thing – if I get knocked out, I can finally rest..."*

# Part I

## The Crisis

# Chapter 2

# My 85-Year-Old Self

At 37, life was good. I had my health, a beautiful family, a career as a management analyst, and a nice side hustle as an adjunct professor.

I'd had a good childhood, too. Loving parents, cool friends, and thirty acres of horse farm to explore on my four-wheeler. The only real blemish: a boy we'll call "Larry."

Larry decided around first grade I'd make a good bully victim. A year younger, scrawny, and conveniently riding the same school bus, he was right. He'd punch me in the leg and call me a puss, flip my ear and frog my arm, always threatening to do more if I protested.

When it first began I couldn't understand why Larry was so mean. Maybe he was lonely. Maybe if I was nice, we could become friends.

As we got older, there were hints he might begin treating me like a person rather than a punching bag. Occasionally he'd get distracted and forget my daily humiliation. But the randomness just made the abuse worse.

Larry never broke a bone or drew blood. And the harassment did taper off as we got older. But in grade school it came most every day, twice a day.

I'd dread it Monday morning, I'd dread it Wednesday afternoon. I even stressed about Larry weekends and summer break.

Over the years I got into a half dozen or so schoolyard scraps against boys my own age and size. But never against Larry. With hundreds of opportunities, the courage never came. I suppose I was conditioned – stuck in a victimhood rut it was hard to escape.

I was ashamed as a boy, and even though I'd grown up, joined the military, started a family and done well for myself, was still ashamed as a man. I didn't obsess over it. But it was always there, just beneath the surface. I'd been a habitual coward, and couldn't forgive myself.

Then in 2014 my favorite college football team lost to their rival for the tenth year in a row. At the end of the game their band played *our* fight song, in *our* stadium. Dejected, I snapped and found myself elbowing my way through groups of the opposing team's fans, and then confronting the other team's drummer – threatening to shove his drumsticks... you know where.

Cooler heads prevailed. But walking away, I couldn't believe what I'd done.

> *"What's wrong with me?* I'm a grown man, a dad. Why am I getting so upset over a game I don't even play?"

The further I walked, the clearer the answer became. I was still haunted by the shame of my childhood, and time was running out to do something about it.

Mike Tyson, of all people, knows how bully shame can eat at you. He's called it a "terminal cancer" you never forget. Here's how Iron Mike dealt with it.

> "I'd be walking with some friends, and I might see one of the guys who beat me up and bullied

me years earlier. He might have gone into a store shopping, and I would drag his [bleep] out of the store and start pummeling him. I didn't even tell my friends why, I'd just say, 'I hate that [bleep] over there,' and they'd jump in too and rip his [bleeping] clothes and beat his [bleeping bleep]. That guy who took my glasses and threw them away? I beat him in the streets like a [bleeping] dog for humiliating me. He may have forgotten about it, but I never did."

I can't say I never fantasized a Tyson-style beatdown on old Larry. But I'm far from Mike Tyson, and in any case know that you can't judge a man for what he did as a boy.

If you could – were I held accountable for all the dumb, mean stuff I did in my teenage years (before the Air Force straightened me out) – I'd have a line of people waiting to get their revenge on *me.* (Belated apologies for the smashed mailboxes, good citizens of Monroe County.)

So I had no plans of tracking down Larry and doing anything to his bleeping bleep. But I still had unfinished business with myself. I couldn't forget, let alone forgive.

Staring down 40, I'd been toying with a midlife crisis redemption idea: box or kickbox, or maybe even do a Mixed Martial Arts fight. I couldn't change the past. But by stepping in the ring now, I could partially redeem it.

Plus, I loved the Rocky movies and the UFC. Actually *doing* that stuff rather than simply watching it? This could be the adventure of a lifetime.

I had no illusions of becoming an MMA champion. I just needed one fight to prove that I could do it – that the kid on that school bus who never fought back was dead and vindicated.

Though I'd been wrestling with the idea for months, I'd been reluctant to say it out loud, let alone do anything about it.

But when I lost my cool with that drummer, the pressure to act swelled. Walking away, I imagined my 85-year-old self looking back over my life:

"You always wanted to fight, but didn't have the guts. You had one life. Now it's too late."

The thought of living out my days without fight footage to watch with my grandkids was terrifying. Despite anything else I'd done or would do, the shame of never redeeming 3rd, 4th, 7th grade me would be unbearable.

The little kid inside needed me to step up and be his hero. And he needed me to do it now.

I'd been a runner since the Air Force, so was in decent shape. But not fighting shape. And while I'd never competed, I'd dabbled in one marital art or another for most of my adult life.

My plan was to amp up my cardio, do a few boxing matches, a kickboxing match, then one MMA fight.

The fact that I wasn't a complete rookie made the idea slightly less crazy. But at 37, it was still pretty nuts.

I suppressed the idea for months before committing the goal to paper. Then in the summer of 2015, I finally mustered the courage to visit a boxing gym and begin my Year of the Fighter.

"Just one MMA fight before I turn 40. *You can do this.*"

# Chapter 3

## 9-11

The first time I suited up for a legit boxing sparring session, the headgear wouldn't fit. It felt floppy, and I was wondering how this banana-shaped thing was supposed to protect my skull. The problem: what I mistook for headgear was a padded jock strap.

Luckily the other boxers were too busy training to notice. My coach, Jesse, whom you'll meet next chapter, explained with a smile, "You're wearing it wrong – that goes down here."

I really should have known better. Though I wouldn't compete until 2016, my martial arts journey had begun fifteen years prior. The reason: 9-11.

I don't think fantasies of averting terrorist plots had anything to do with it. 9-11 was more a reminder that life can end in an instant, which spurred me to go ahead and do martial arts rather than simply dreaming about it. I'm sure bully victim shame was a motivator then, too, even if I wasn't ready to admit it.

My first art was Silat, an Indonesian style rumored to have been developed by cannibals. The techniques tended to focus on hyperextending joints and otherwise maiming, which is helpful when your goal isn't to simply to beat your opponent, but to possibly eat him.

We practiced a balance drill called "push hands" (slow Sumo Wrestling in a smaller circle) as well as a counterstriking exercise called "sticky hands" that sounds messier than it is.

The class included a little Kung Fu, as well as a "Ba Gua" warm-up – a fluid sequence that looks and feels like Tai Chi for assassins. And though I never made it that far, I'm told students graduating into Phase Four learned how to sauté human flesh. Kidding!

Despite the dark undertones, Silat proved an inviting intro to the world of self-defense. Sifu Richard Clear was an excellent first instructor (smart, patient), and many of the principles he taught would serve me well.

I'd probably been studying Silat for a year when I bumped into a friend's older brother at a Toughman Contest in nearby Sweetwater. Dennis had dabbled in various arts in his younger days, and had decided only one was worth his time: Jiu Jitsu. He invited me to his place to show me firsthand.

On puzzle-piece wrestling mats in his living room, Dennis taught me the ground fighting positions of mount, side mount and guard, basic arm bars and chokes, and even a few Judo throws.

Though it was awkward getting *that* up close and personal with another dude, I learned fast why Royce Gracie dominated the early UFCs: it's hard to fight back when you're being choked unconscious.

Dennis talked me into training with his old instructor in an actual gym. It would be a 45-minute drive up towards the airport, but we'd carpool.

Dr. Carter was (and remains) a gentle giant. A wrestling and Judo champion, martial arts had been a way to channel his natural aggression, and an opportunity to mentor.

I enjoyed the Jiu Jitsu submissions more than the Judo throws, which I found tough to pull off against larger opponents. But "rolling" (Jiu Jitsu sparring) messed with my head. I often left class fuzzy, not just because I was exhausted, but from the clinching and straining. Being "blood choked" as Dennis called it probably wasn't the healthiest thing for my brain.

One night a wrestler survivalist guy named Andrew came to class. No one but Dr. Carter could touch him – he was smearing students at will. He wasn't a jerk about it. If you were slow and careful, he returned the favor. But if you got cocky, he'd crank up the intensity, and soon you were tapping out (submitting, giving up).

Andrew kept coming back, and once we had swapped enough sweat he invited me to join a new "combatives" training group. Combatives is essentially Mixed Martial Arts with weapons, plus no-frills, to-the-point, unarmed techniques (think soft targets: eyes, throat, groin). I agreed, we decided to meet Sunday afternoons at that same dojo, and dubbed ourselves "Integrated Defense Systems."

A freckled wrestler named Jeff joined, and so did Chuck, a heavyset firearms enthusiast engineer. We trained in boxing, kickboxing, wrestling and Jiu Jitsu, all with and without weapons, which enabled me to see how much I preferred hitting sweaty men than rolling around on the ground with them.

Even though I had more training in ground fighting, anytime we'd work focus mit combos (one guy holds pads and calls out boxing/kickboxing combinations; the other guy hits them) or do light sparring (box or kickbox), I was happiest.

There was something instinctually gratifying about punching guys in the face, even when they were bigger and punching back. Plus, what boy of the 80s didn't dream of being Rocky? I'd hum his theme song as I trained:

"Bum bum, bah bah bah, *bah bah bah,* bah bah bah..."

An experimental group, if an expert offered a self-defense solution, we'd try it. My nickname became "Master Shredder" because I liked Rich Dimitri's mauling, biting "shredder" technique so much (look him up – vicious stuff).

We also practiced weapons disarms with plastic guns and knives, finding that a lot of the flashy techniques you see in movies wouldn't work against an uncooperative opponent. Jeff would be trying to take the knife, Chuck would be trying to keep it – if this were for real they'd both be bloody messes. But by resisting we figured out what was legit and what wasn't.

The "Room of Doom" drill was a sadistic favorite. We'd put on MMA gloves (light knuckle padding with open finger holes for grappling) and prop up wrestling pads to form an 8x8 enclosure. Andrew would choose a plastic weapon, enter and hide, and one of us would have to go in and try to disarm him.

Sometimes we'd dim the lights or make the second guy go in with his eyes closed and not open them until the first blow was thrown. I was usually the smallest, least experienced person there, so for me this drill tended to suck. But were I the biggest and baddest, I wouldn't have learned anything.

I'd trained in some multiple-attackers stuff in Silat, much of which we confirmed was good. For example, if confronted by two or more opponents,

16

realize you are not Bruce Lee, and throw your wallet in one direction and run in the other. If the bait and run trick doesn't work, line your opponents up and fight them one at a time. Where you don't want to be is between them, where one bad guy can occupy your attention while the others smash your face. Easier said than done, but lining them up is the goal.

School and workplace shootings had become a worry, and based on our tests, the best way to handle a lone active shooter was not to hide under your desk and wait to be executed, but to tell the three strongest people in the room to crouch single file inside the main door. As the bad guy enters, the first person's job is to grab the gun and point it in a safe direction (at the shooter will suffice); the second person's job is to tackle or otherwise take the shooter to the ground; the third person's job is to kick the shooter in the head until they die.

Killing an opponent, even an active shooter, was the opposite of what Dr. Carter taught. His goal was to be *so* proficient that he wouldn't have to harm the other guy to stop him. That's why he liked Judo throws so much. With enough skill, you have the option to provide a soft landing. And while a Jiu Jitsu choke can kill, it can also just put a guy to sleep.

His most important training rule: take care of your partner. His most important self-defense rule: show compassion and restraint.

My own approach became a mix: be compassionate when you enjoy the luxury, but ruthless when necessary, such as against really big, armed or multiple attackers.

Before my first child, I was training combatives Sundays, Jiu Jitsu and Judo Tuesdays and Thursdays, with periodic field trips to the range or woods on Saturdays with IDS. But priorities change. Not only do kids want to spend time with their dads, good dads want to spend time with their kids.

Three days per week became two, then one, then sometime during graduate school I put a Spar Pro boxing dummy in my garage and decided hitting him was enough for the time being.

So my Year of the Fighter didn't happen in a vacuum. I'd been thinking about it. I'd even trained a little. I just hadn't mustered the guts to go all the way.

# Part II

## Monroe County Boxing Club

# Chapter 4

# The Moving Punching Bag

An hour south of my family's horse farm was Indian Boundary – the "crown jewel" of the Cherokee National Forest.

Pristine lake with panoramic mountain views, sandy beach, three-mile biking trail around the shore, picnic tables and campsites – we frequented when I was a kid, and it remains one of my favorite places on the planet.

The nearest town: Tellico Plains.

Poke Byers had moved to Tellico from Oklahoma in the 70s, bringing his family's boxing tradition with him. As a result, dozens (probably hundreds) of mountain boys got a chance to learn the sweet science at Tellico Boxing Club. None were more talented, dedicated or successful than Poke's son, Jesse.

I'd first met Jesse at a party when we were teenagers. My parents were going through a divorce, Dad had moved out, Mom and my sister were taking horses camping, and with the house to myself, I'd invited a few friends over for a bonfire kegger.

Word spread, and pretty soon Doeskin Valley Farm was overrun. How people found that dead-end road in the dark in the age before GPS, I don't know. But they came from all four corners of Monroe County, including Tellico Plains.

I was making the rounds introducing myself when a blonde in my driveway caught my eye. Before I could say hi, a friend pulled me aside:

"Hey, that's Jesse 'Cool Hands' Byers's girlfriend."

Never mind...

Jesse, a few feet away with a group of friends, didn't look especially tough. But his reputation preceded him. If you're going to flirt with another man's girlfriend, make sure he's not a nationally ranked fighter.

Jesse had been boxing from the time he could square up, but it wasn't until he found himself in and out of trouble as a young man that he got serious.

My mom's told me, "The Bible says if you raise a kid right they may stray, but they'll eventually come home." Poke called this "The God Trap." And when it sprung on Jesse, Poke was waiting.

Who knew a kid from little old Tellico Plains could win a national Golden Gloves title? Or fight (and beat) Oscar Diaz on Fox Sports? Or go toe-to-toe with Floyd "Money" Mayweather for three rounds?

Jesse even gave pro fighting a shot, but in the end decided joining his dad's painting business was the adult thing to do.

A couple of decades later, probably about the same time I was embarrassing myself at that football game, Jesse (now a co-coach at the gym) and Poke were planning to move their boxing operation to Madisonville, the county seat, by converting an indoor batting facility into Monroe County Boxing Club.

A Christian outreach gym, kids and adults intending to compete would train for free. They put scripture on the walls, the jump rope platforms, and the club t-shirts:

"If God is for us, who can be against us?"

This was the Byers' way of bettering the community and saving souls, a place for youth and adults alike to regroup and recommit when life got off track.

So I was in good hands when I decided to begin my midlife crisis run at MCBC. Jesse and Poke were not only excellent coaches, but good men. They knew how to box, knew how to turn a fish into a fighter, and were doing it for all the right reasons. Their gentle encouragement to live a more Godly life didn't hurt either.

When I climbed into the ring for my first real sparring session (after replacing my jock strap hat with actual headgear), I was what my soon-to-be friend Jamey called a "moving punching bag." Stiff, slow, easily winded. It wasn't pretty. I asked Jesse how he thought I might do in a real bout.

"A lot depends on who you fight."

This was a nice way of saying I'd get my ass handed to me. But I was willing to put in the work.

After the typical 45-minute warm up circuit of jumping rope, shadowboxing and hitting the heavy bags, I'd go a round with Jamey, then a round with his 16-year-old offensive lineman son Kaiden, then another round with Jamey. Both were a handful, but Jamey was "open," meaning he had competed in more than ten official fights, and was sanctioned to fight other open fighters.

Jamey must have thought I was crazy, an almost 40-year-old philosophy professor competing for the first time. I told him I had always wanted to, but never had the guts. He seemed to respect that.

I suspect he also thought showing mercy in the ring wouldn't do me any favors. The better our sparring simulated an actual fight, the better prepared I'd be when my time came.

He wanted the same for his son.

"Press him," he'd yell when I'd spar with Kaiden. "Don't go easy on him."

The other top competitor at the gym was 19-year-old Triston. Second to only Jamey in skill, he exceeded his mercilessness. Triston was a natural predator, and if you looked tired, or backed down and tried to rest, he would pounce. Sometimes he'd punctuate hooks with *"Hep, hep!"* as if to drown out your groans.

Basketball players can rest when they get tired. You bring the ball up court slowly, give your man some space, call a timeout. In Jiu Jitsu, in the right position, you can chill and catch your breath. At the time I thought boxers had no way to recover. You get tired, the other guy sees it and takes you out.

I know because I used to wait for 20-something sparring partner Orlando to wear down. We'd both go hard in rounds 1 and 2. But round 3 was when he became my moving punching bag.

I learned later how to form a shield with my forearms and minimize damage. If you watch the pros, they'll put their fists on their forehead, bring their elbows in, and weather a storm.

That's how Ali beat Foreman, his "rope-a-dope" strategy.

"Go ahead, wear yourself out. Now it's *my* turn."

But back then, sparring Triston, I thought head movement was the defensive key. And it might have been were I naturally fast like Jamey. But I was not.

Exhaustion meant praying for the bell while he drummed my temple. One session in particular, I ate some really hard shots. Winded, defenseless, having to listen to that *"Hep! Hep!"* while getting dizzier with each punch, it was a miracle I didn't fall down.

When the round finally ended I was so dejected I said, *"Gosh darnit"* as I climbed out of the ring. Except, I didn't say gosh darnit.

Jesse, owner and head coach of this fine Christian establishment, was standing right there. He didn't say a word. He just looked straight ahead. Another victim went in, I took my gloves off and moved to the back of the pack, still dizzy, still disgusted.

A less measured, less diplomatic man might have lost his temper, might have asked me to leave, might have made an example of me in front of the younger boxers. Instead, Jesse waited until we were cleaning up to approach me alone.

"You know, anytime I'm frustrated I'll ask God to help me. The Lord can give me strength, calm me down, help me better deal with things."

I thanked him for his testimony, but I was really thanking him for being the bigger man. I suspected he'd had his own bell rung a few times and could relate.

In any case, that was the last time I cursed in Monroe County Boxing Club. Jesse and Poke had taken me in, agreed to coach me (for free), and I'd disrespected them and their gym. Jesse had shown mercy and restraint, and I owed him.

# Chapter 5

## Singh

As the beatings continued, my skill and stamina improved. I started landing my own shots on Triston, though usually just hard jabs. And I found that Jamey and Kaiden didn't hit back as much when I kept busy hitting them. One class Jamey asked:

"Are you going to Knoxville Friday to spar?"

Frank Eppolito of Eppolito Boxing Gym was inviting local fighters to practice against his team.

"Yeah – I'm not scared."

This meant I was terrified. I was still getting beat up at MCBC, but at least I knew which guys I could and couldn't handle.

Sparring at a completely different gym against completely different fighters? In the big city? I'm sure Jamey could tell I was intimidated. But he didn't poke fun – he was simply supportive.

It was October 10th, 2015 – just over a year since the drummer boy incident that set all this in motion. The team met at the gym to ride up together in the club van. I snuck into the bathroom, locked the door, and leaned close to the mirror.

"You're scared, but you're gonna suck it up and fight. You wanted this – now go get it."

On the way up Poke and Jesse were joking with some of the boxers about their fight names. There was James "Hurricane" Heaton, who fought with a wild flurry of punches, Triston "Too Late" Jenkins, who once you thought about dodging, it was already too late. Poke asked me:

"What's your fight name going to be?"

"Midlife Crisis. Matt 'Midlife Crisis' Deaton."

"I like it."

I was usually the oldest active boxer in the room. Jamey was in his early thirties, Orlando his twenties. But everyone else was twenty or below – most in high school, some in junior high.

Then when we got to Frank's gym I met Singh, a retired Army Ranger turned spiritualist vlogger.

"Creation of an Elder Beast" I found out later was his YouTube tagline.

Singh had a steady, shuffling style, accentuated by his footwear: sandals. The other boxers, and the other coaches, had never seen anything like him. Boxers aren't supposed to move like... *that.* They're not supposed to have a grey beard. They're definitely not supposed to wear sandals.

Frank first matched me with a couple of younger guys my size. After going hard with Jamey and Triston at MCBC, they didn't give me much trouble.

I'd taken my gloves off and was ready to head south when he asked if I wanted to go one more round, this time with Singh.

I was anxious to wrap up and leave. I'd survived my first sparring outing. Let's take this van back to Monroe County and call it a weekend. But I wasn't going to puss out in front of the team.

I probably weighed 155 at the time, Singh maybe 210. We were both old by boxing standards, but he was in his 50s, not his late 30s. Singh looked pretty solid though, so Jesse was advising I use my likely stamina and mobility advantages to dance and keep him back with jabs.

The strategy worked at first. But it wasn't natural. Stiff and upright, I felt like Glass Joe from Mike Tyson's Punchout. (In case you're not a Nintendo buff, Glass Joe was not a good fighter.)

One thing I learned about myself fighting: I'm most comfortable tackling problems head-on. Dancing and delaying just aren't my style.

When I inevitably went in to swap licks with special forces sandals grandpa, I landed a few punches, but his landed harder, and a solid right opened a cut on the bridge of my nose.

I survived, and was proud for accepting that final round. I was even proud of the cut. Frank applied some Liquid Stitch, and I was good to go.

My first out of town sparring match was complete. It was a heck of a difference from where I had been only a year before, a sports fan pathetically threatening the other team's poor drummer. No longer a spectator, I was the one in the arena now, and it felt great – cut nose and all.

And while odd by East Tennessee standards, Singh turned out to be pretty cool. Super friendly, and probably the only other person in the building who'd practiced "push hands," that balance drill from my Silat days.

I found out later that he was training at Frank's in preparation to open a new MMA gym in Morristown. He'd written a book on mixing Eastern techniques into boxing, and had actually been an MMA instructor since 2006.

Looking back, Singh was taking it easy on me that night. He didn't have anything to prove. That solid right was just a friendly reminder to keep my guard up. Advanced fighters will often show newbies mercy like that. There's no reason to dominate when you *know* you could take a guy out.

But fights between competitors of similar experience are another story. Vulnerable, unproven, with the added pressure of a live audience – they're in it to win it, and know one must do poorly for the other to do well.

And so I would receive no such mercy five months later at my very first bout.

# Chapter 6

# No Fear

March 11<sup>th</sup>, 2016

I'm at Ace Miller's Golden Gloves Gym in Knoxville. It's been seventeen months since I threatened that drummer at a football game.

Poke's wrapping my wrists for my first fight. I. Am. Nervous.

I was nervous in the team van. I was nervous during weigh-ins. I was nervous during the pre-fight medical check.

"*How* old are you?" the doctor asked while removing my blood pressure cuff.

"Almost 40."

"And what are you doing here?"

"Midlife crisis."

<...silence...>

A couple of hours before my match I caught a glimpse of my opponent, Denzel, a kid no more than 20. I walked over and introduced myself.

I learned this was his home gym, and confirmed this would be his first fight as well.

A non-boxer friend beside him – a country boy in a camo hat – was giving me a puzzled stare. He finally asked the question he'd been holding.

"Mister, *how* old are you?"

Denzel didn't seem interested in chatting. Maybe he was weirded out about fighting his dad. Then I saw Poke giving me a look so I excused myself to see what was up.

"What are you doing?"

"Just talking to my opponent."

"You can make friends with that kid *after* the fight."

With the transport and the pre-fight checks, I felt like a cow being prepped for slaughter. The long wait between weigh-ins and the bouts was the worst. But as the sun went down the crowd rolled in, the matches finally began.

The gym only had four pairs of official fight gloves, so I didn't get gloved up until the match before mine was underway. My hands slid in easily – the boxers before had them warm and sweaty for me.

Jesse took me aside to do a few combos. He was eying Denzel and his coach. They were talking rather than hitting, probably studying my form. As soon as Denzel started on his mits, Jesse saw something.

"Alright, he's a southpaw."

I thought, *"Oh shit* – I've never even sparred a southpaw."

He tried to give me some quick tips on how to handle left-handed fighters.

"Use your right cross – it's going to be open."

But it was too late to adjust. My skill and style were my skill and style, and I'd just have to do my best with what I had.

Finding out Denzel was a southpaw brought my nervousness to a head. But as the fight before ours ended and we were called to the ring, my confidence began to grow.

As I walked closer to the ring, it expanded. With each step up to the platform, it rose. And as I reached the top and slipped between the ropes, my anxiety dissolved.

In its place: determination, resolve, and something I'd been suppressing – anger.

This guy was here to beat me up in front of all these people. That pissed me off. Breaching the ropes, I was born anew. Southpaw or not, let's go.

We both started tight. I'd found success with my jab sparring, so I used it. More shots were landing than I had expected. Some left-right combos as well.

Denzel was elusive, all over the ring, side-skipping along the outside as I followed. I spent most of my time chasing him.

He was also bending at the waist like no one I'd faced, slipping way under my punches. If I'd known what I was doing I might have uppercut him. But that's the one punch I hadn't practiced.

Sparring, time went by super slow.

"When will the freaking bell ring so Triston will stop cracking my skull..."

But I was amazed at how quickly a two-minute round flew by in a real fight. Too fast to get much done, but not fast enough to keep from getting tired.

Sooner than expected the bell rang and the ref pointed us to our corners. In mine was Poke positioning a stool.

"Sit down."

I complied. Jesse hopped into the ring and began toweling off sweat.

Poke reached in and pulled out my mouthpiece, and replaced it with a squirt of water. He grabbed a white bucket and held it in front of me.

"Spit."

They were both trying to give me tips – stuff on how to cut off the ring and better deal with the southpaw thing. But for all their coaching, I was too absorbed in the moment – all I could think was:

*"It's like I'm Rocky!* I get to spit in a bucket and everything!"

In the second round our punches grew loopier, our defenses sloppier, and our legs wobblier.

By the third we were both drowning. It's hard to see in the smartphone video of the fight, but both of us were gasping for air, eyes rolling with lightheadedness – not from punches, but exhaustion.

In my case part of the cause was that my mouthpiece didn't have an air channel. With my chin down and teeth clinched – the way you're supposed to fight to protect your jaw – I had to breathe through my nose.

Have you ever tried sprinting while breathing only through your nose? While someone's punching that same nose? Not fun.

The $15 upgrade to a "Shock Doctor" afterwards was well worth it. But in this first fight I was stuck with the introductory suffocation model.

An entry from my journal, recorded the day after the fight summed it up:

*Denzel was tired, very tired, especially in the third round. But he kept going, throwing some decent combos, and landing some hard shots. I was tired too, and was breathing with my mouth open (damn, I did that a LOT – way more than in sparring), and at least twice got my mouthpiece rattled around and had to fix it with my tongue. At one point I thought, "Man, it would have been bad if he had knocked that out..."*

The fight ended, and the decision went to the judges.

I'd been the aggressor, I'd better controlled the center of the ring, and I'd landed at least as many shots as Denzel, so was pretty sure I'd won. I was even more sure in the final seconds when the ref gave Denzel some sort of warning, though I wasn't sure for what.

I thought, "My first fight and I'm going home with a victory. Heck yeah."

But the judges had seen it differently. A split decision – instead of my hand, the ref raised Denzel's.

Poke and Jesse insisted I had won. So did the ref. Escorting me out of the ring he said under his breath:

"I thought *you* won."

"Me too."

The team didn't warn me beforehand, but it's apparently hard to win at the other guy's home gym with anything short of a knockout or referee stoppage.

But it was all good. The post-fight ringside doc cleared me fast, but was still examining my opponent's pupils for signs of a concussion three or four minutes into the next match. We'd rocked each other for sure. But I'd rocked him a little harder.

Plus, slipping through those ropes without fear – that was my victory. I went to bed that night with an imaginary championship belt around my waist.

I smiled about it the rest of that evening, I'm smiling about it right now, and I suspect 85-year-old me will be smiling still. If you see me in a nursing home around 2067, do me a favor and read this journal entry aloud:

42

*It was an awesome experience: being one of the fighters amongst the audience beforehand, getting my hands taped and "gloved up," stepping through the ropes and under the lights, sitting on a stool and spitting into a bucket during the breaks (just like in the movies), slugging it out for three solid rounds, and shaking lots of supportive fans' hands afterwards.*

The next fight was to be hosted by my gym, at the high school in my hometown. *The Monroe County Rumble.*

# Chapter 7

# The Rumble

I'd proven to myself I was tough enough. Now I had the chance to prove it to neighbors, classmates, maybe even kids on that school bus who'd seen me wimp out all those years before. Never mind that they were grown and unlikely to remember, let alone care. I remembered. I cared.

I got the word out. Anyone with $10 and an interest, be at Sequoyah High Saturday night. Matt "Midlife Crisis" Deaton is gonna fight.

But in amateur boxing it doesn't matter how eager you are. You need an opponent of similar weight and experience willing to risk a fight on your turf. Jesse worked the phones, calling coaches within driving distance to see if they might have a willing boxer.

I'd played in an alumni basketball game a couple of years prior. We had too many people for that. Old Blue Devils had to ride the bench for their chance to relive hardwood glory.

But another 140-pounder with less than ten fights? The early word was that a boxer with six fights out of Georgia was in. But then Monday, Tuesday, Wednesday went by with no confirmation. Wednesday night, I'd pretty much given up, said forget about maintaining my fighting weight and eaten sodium-rich salsa and chips before bed.

Then Thursday, I got a text from Jesse.

"I've got you matched with a 132-pounder out of Alabama. Can you meet him at 136?"

I checked the scale: 142.

The boxing gym was hot that evening. I mean H-O-T hot. Poke would say, "That's why we don't have a bunch of parents in here complaining about how we're training their kids. It's too hot for them." This was a good thing for a man trying to cut weight.

By the time I was home from the gym that night I'd dropped to 136. Water weight, I'm sure. But 6 pounds in a day is still 6 pounds in a day. Remember this if you have weight loss goals. Pounds lost do not always equate to fat burnt. But at a boxing weigh-in, it's all the same.

So I'd made weight and just needed to maintain it for a couple of days. I didn't feel my best, but if this is what I needed to weigh to fight in the Rumble, this is what I'd weigh.

Then Friday Jesse left a voicemail.

"This guy's coach is flaky... I've never worked with him before... It's not looking good."

All that training, sweating, stress and excitement, and probably my only chance to box in front of my hometown, evaporating.

Even though I'd only had one fight, I was willing to take the mystery boxer out of Georgia with six fights who fell through. But this Alabama kid who Jesse found on Thursday only had one bout. With my prior martial arts experience, dozens of sparring sessions, and a real match under my belt, I was convinced I'd eat him alive, underweight or not.

But it wasn't to be.

I went to the Rumble anyway to support the team. An old Air Force buddy, Ron, came with his wife Holly. Having to explain why I was in the stands rather than fighting sucked. They'd seen my Knoxville fight online. Was I afraid to fight in front of people I knew live?

With a taste of the action, it was tough being demoted to spectator again. But two events really made the night special.

First, Jamey had recently opened up about his past. He'd mentioned taking a long break from boxing, and I hadn't asked why. The reason: prison.

A natural athlete, Jamey had been a star running back in elementary school. He was fast. Scary fast. *"Who's that little white blur?"* fast.

Then in the 7th grade he developed chronic knee pain. No longer the fastest, his popularity and self-esteem took a hit, and he turned to substance abuse: alcohol then weed.

A couple of years into high school his knees were better, but the bad habits remained. He switched to a vocational track to graduate, and played well enough to earn a football scholarship. It was in college that Jamey got his first opportunity to sell drugs. He found that he was naturally good at that, too.

A drug dealer's life doesn't mesh well with the demands of higher education. And when the college experiment failed, the downward spiral accelerated. Jail time became prison time, and winning $50k from a scratch-off lottery ticket just made things worse.

Convicts can be sheepish about admitting their past, especially to management analyst ethics professor types. So to make Jamey more comfortable, I shared my own story.

Right about the time my parents were splitting, I got a driver's license and a job. While they were busy arguing, I was free to skip school, party, rebel.

Good times, except I rebelled a little too much the summer after high school, and found myself in a pink concrete cell – the place Monroe County sends punk teenagers who've had one too many Zima, especially when they loiter at the Magic Mart and yell profanities at the police. (For those who don't know, Zima was an ultra-manly beverage popular in the mid-90s, reserved for only the manliest of men.)

I'd gotten into plenty of trouble at school (vandalism, skipping class), but for all my mailbox-bashing hooliganism, had always stayed one step ahead of the cops. I was confident I'd get away this time as I had dozens of times before.

When the officer ordered me to recite the alphabet and stumble in a straight line, I thought,

"He'll never actually take me to jail for loitering in a gas station parking lot…"

But once it was clear those potent Zimas had me over the limit, he moved out of interrogation mode and into arrest mode. While he was patting me down I warned him,

"Watch out – I've got a hard-on!"

This did not help my case.

As he was putting me in the back of the squad car, it still didn't seem real. I thought he was just going to take me down the road to scare me, then turn me loose.

"Next time drink your Zima at home, kid."

Nope. This time was for real.

When we got to the station, my handcuffs wouldn't accept the key, so they had to call for a jailer to break them with bolt cutters.

Who got the honor? The father of my first elementary school girlfriend, the girl who'd given me my first (cheek) kiss. I knew her dad was a cop, and had seen him at Christmas plays and whatnot. Who knew we'd meet again like this.

> "Conard, right? Hey, I used to date your daughter!"

He was not amused.

Did you know they confiscate your shoelaces, I guess so you can't hang yourself? Or that the drunk tank commode is metal and in the middle of the room?

That Pepto Bismol pink room was busy on a Saturday night. Surrounded by men in their 30s and 40s, I could see that they were my future if things didn't change. So I decided to do what my dad, a Navy vet, had been encouraging me to do for months, and join the Air Force. One of the best decisions of my life.

Twenty years later, everything had worked out happily ever after – a fancy college degree, true love, great kids. I'd just needed a wakeup call. In my mid-thirties I actually tracked down that cop and thanked him. If he hadn't busted me then, maybe I'd be in a cell right now.

While a night in the Monroe County drunk tank isn't state prison, Jamey and I could be reformed jailbirds together. Jesse, too.

Jamey, knowing I'd written a public speaking book and did occasional keynotes, approached me a couple of weeks before the Rumble. He was living soberly for the first time in a long time and wanted to share his story, possibly by speaking to local inmates. But as intimidated as I had been by fighting, he was intimidated by public speaking.

I of course agreed to coach him. He'd been coaching me in his area of expertise. It was only fair that I repay the favor.

A few days later he brought highlights of his rise, fall and recovery handwritten on three sheets of notebook paper. I read about his knee problems, his downturn, and the blown lottery winnings.

I also read how, on top of twenty-five sanctioned boxing matches, he'd been in another twenty-two street fights. He'd faced forty-seven charges and spent five years behind bars. But today, he insisted, he was a new creature.

> "I'm a big baby now. Still get mad, but handle it much better. I care about people now. I can love them."

He had a powerful message, and the street cred to get guys facing similar struggles to listen.

The bad news was that he was a complete speaking rookie. Organizing his ideas and getting him comfortable delivering them would take work. But there was no rush.

Then the week of the Rumble he called.

> "Hey, I asked Jesse if I could deliver my testimony during intermission Saturday and he said yes. Can you help me get ready?"

I think this was Wednesday. Not much time at all. And this presentation wouldn't be for a half dozen inmates. It would be for a gymnasium full of people. But I agreed and went to work.

We spoke several times that Thursday and Friday. His message would focus on the three things that had helped him find hope and stability: boxing, family and Jesus. I encouraged him to rehearse, just like in the boxing gym.

> "No one ever got good at a 1-2 combo without practice, and the same is true for public speaking. It takes doing it over and over."

I told him another trick is to visualize, which he knew all about from shadowboxing.

I was embarrassed to shadowbox when I first started training. You look silly, fighting an imaginary opponent. But I learned the more realistic your visualization, the more intense your practice, the more successful you'll be when the opponent's real. Only actual fights and sparring did more to advance me as a fighter. I told Jamey the same was true with public speaking.

> "Imagine the audience exactly as you expect – supportive, attentive, eager to hear what you have to say – and yourself confidently delivering exactly as you desire. The more realistic your simulation, the better prepared

you'll be come show time. I'll sometimes speak to stuffed animals in my living room before a big presentation. Whatever it takes."

He practiced as I asked, but when I saw him at the Rumble he looked about as nervous as I did before my first fight – like he was the one being prepped for slaughter.

I wanted to give him some last-minute encouragement, but it was crowded, the fights began, and we got separated before I had a chance. But I found him right before intermission.

"Fake it 'til you make it."

We'd talked about this. It meant that if he was nervous (and he was), to pretend to be confident until the genuine confidence kicked in. It worked.

His talk wasn't perfect, but he held the attention of a couple of hundred people for seven or so minutes, and even got a little mid-talk applause. It was nice to see people I knew were special to him – his kids, coaches Jesse and Poke – looking on with admiration.

He finished to cheers and was greeted by a half dozen people congratulating him for the fantastic job. I didn't want to take anything away from his moment, so I stayed in my seat. But he came by about ten minutes later with a beaming smile and thanks.

The second cool thing that made the Rumble worthwhile: teammate Nathan Littrel.

Nathan happened to be a personal trainer, and was a tough sparring partner.

Tense, with contact lenses that sometimes fell (or got knocked) out, he was one of our physically strongest fighters. His combos didn't always land. But when they did, they were jarring. If he could learn to slip and follow up, this guy would be dangerous.

Nathan had fought his first fight the same night as mine, only he'd been paired against a fighter who was darn close to being open. The tradeoff was that this guy had dropped a couple of weight classes.

I guess the thought was that while Nathan lacked experience, his athleticism meant he should be able to hang with a more seasoned fighter who might be weaker having cut significant weight.

That this was a bad idea became apparent fast. Nathan's opponent had the skill, speed, experience and strength, while Nathan only had the strength.

The loss, which ended by referee stoppage, was a blow to Nathan's ego. It would have been to anyone's. But as a personal trainer, he took it harder. I could see it that night in Knoxville, and I could see it was still haunting him at the Rumble.

Even more than it would have been for me, this was Nathan's chance at redemption, but also a risk. He invited friends, family, coworkers, and even reserved a ringside table so his crew could see the fight up close. Would his second bout end as his first, the referee calling off the beating? Only this time in front of his hometown?

Nathan left absolutely no doubt who the better boxer was. From bell to bell he fought like a man with a lot to prove, and dominated. As the two stood on either side of the referee awaiting the judges' decision, it was clear to everyone in the building that Nathan had won. That is, to everyone but Nathan.

From the bleachers I could see his lingering doubt. He'd mopped the floor with this guy, but he hadn't shaken that loss. But when his arm was lifted in victory, his relief and joy were palpable. Congrats, Nathan!

I was happy for Nate, but also jealous. Reviewing the lineup, there were actually two 140-pound boxers on the card. Why couldn't I have been matched against one of them instead of the guys who wound up backing out?

Watching their fight, both seemed timid, didn't push the pace, and didn't look in the best shape.

There are thousands of boxers who could have drilled me that night. But watching those two, I was certain I'd have been the one doing the drilling.

Part of me was ashamed for lusting to embarrass an unworthy opponent. But that just comes with the nature of boxing. You respect the other guy, and after it's over you can be friends. But in the moment, you're both vulnerable, and you both know that for one of you to do well the other must do poorly. There are few win-wins in boxing.

But that night belonged to Jamey and Nathan. Mine would come a month later.

# Chapter 8

# Johnson City

Having sat through the Rumble, I was hungry. My next opportunity would be May 21ˢᵗ in Johnson City, two and a half hours from home in the northeast tip of the state.

That week I felt and looked great. Thanks to the new mouthpiece I could actually breathe. Jamey noticed how much my stamina had improved sparring.

"Use your endurance as a weapon. That guy won't know what to think Saturday when you just keep coming."

The morning of the fight I headed out for my usual 5k jog to Rasar Landing boat dock and back. There aren't too many runners on Corntassel Road, let alone boxers. But locals were used to me by then, and knew not to run me over.

I was feeling weak for some reason so I tried a visualization trick I'd used before.

I pictured a black stallion my dad had ridden to an Amateur World Grand Championship at Racking and Halter when I was a boy.

Black September or "Pepper," as we called him, pulsated with power standing still. But toward the end of a horse show the organ cadence would pick up, the crowd would cheer louder, and Pepper would lay his ears back, kick into high gear, and rack right past the competition – eyes wide, nostrils flaring.

Running, I could usually get a second wind by pretending to do the same. But this morning something was off.

When I got back, I went a few rounds on a Muay Thai heavy bag my old combatives buddy Andrew had donated. Andrew had conquered his own midlife crisis fight challenge (which had doubled as divorce therapy) five years' prior, winning two of two MMA fights before retiring into fatherhood.

Andrew knew why I had to fight, knew what it took, and so lent me some wrestling mindset and neurolinguistics programming books.

The basic upshot of the wrestling books: being a fighter is tough, but suck it up and press forward – don't be a puss. And rather than always worrying about your weaknesses, build on your strengths. Shoring up liabilities may make you well-rounded. But amplifying strengths makes you *dangerous.*

The upshot of the neurolinguistics books: self-coaching is absolutely essential. Record affirmations on paper, recite them before you go to bed, as soon as you get up, in the shower. Become the person you aspire to be by first embracing the vision in your mind, then making it your reality. Here's one of the affirmations I wrote in my fight notebook:

> "I am a battle beast... I love hardcore battle training. Exhaustion is simply a barrier to push through. My body *will* respond when I need it. I am more technically skilled, faster, and stronger than my opponent, and he will learn to respect me."

The books were a nice complement to the technical coaching and spiritual encouragement at the boxing gym. I'd also done some research online.

61

There was this Expert Boxing guy with clear YouTube tutorials. And I'd been watching Manny Pacquiao's training footage. Pac Man's combos were fast, *"Who's that little white blur?"* fast. Since I was small like him, I started punching faster.

I also looked up some old Tyson vids. When I was a kid, he was just the guy who would knock people out. (Little did I know he'd been bullied, too.) But now I could study and appreciate his technique.

Tyson was a master of putting his bodyweight behind his fists. He'd crouch waaaay down and twist into his uppercuts, pushing from the ground up with ferocious power, with "bad intentions" as his coach Cus D'Amato used to say.

Had Tyson relied on the strength of his arms, he'd have never made it out of Catskill. But his full body power combined with his ability to change direction and follow explosive hooks with explosive crosses is what left so many opponents unconscious.

Years prior, my Silat instructor had tried to teach me that waist power = striking power. The slow motion sparring and Ba Gua were to build fluidity, and to teach us how to use our bodies as connected weapons.

Bruce Lee taught the same, that quality martial arts technique flows from our core. Poke called this "sitting down" on your punches.

"Sit down on that right," he'd yell.

That morning I knew in my head that bending my knees and twisting in the direction I was hitting would add power to my punches. I knew I could and should go faster like Pac Man. But translating that knowledge into my own performance was proving tough. I wrote in my journal:

*Of all the days to be "off," please don't let it be today. I've felt like a champ all week at the gym. Don't let today be the day my body decides to take a break.*

Different from my first fight, at this weigh-in boxers were expected to strip down to their undies, just like in the big UFC matches. Except we were fighting for pride and kicks, not a paycheck, and were weighing in a backstage locker room, not in front of reporters.

One of my teenage teammates, Brayden, said it was too bad I wasn't getting to show off my six pack.

"I'd be intimidated if my opponent had abs like yours."

Getting down to 140 pounds hadn't been easy, but it did make for a defined physique. I'd often tell my wife with a wink:

"Enjoy this boxer's body while you can. It's not going to last forever."

Jesse and Poke drove us to Chick-fil-A to fuel up. Boy, can starving boxers eat some chicken. The more I ate, and the more I hydrated, the better I felt.

Once back at the venue I found a quiet spot by some vending machines in the lobby and shadowboxed. Spectators entering at the other end could see my middle aged self fighting an imaginary opponent, which was a little embarrassing. But I didn't care. I was a real fighter – never mind my age. And the more I moved, the better I felt. Maybe that morning I was just hungry.

Soon our first fighters were gloving up, and the bouts were starting.

Five minutes before my match Jamey took me back out by the vending machines to warm up on the mits. He could tell I was hot.

Hydrated and full of chicken, that morning's sluggishness was gone. I was far from Tyson. But I was close to my personal peak.

"You're ready."

Not to brag, but I was. With that first fight out of the way, I now knew how fast an actual bout went by, how I wasn't going to get embarrassed, how I could hold my own. And I had that new mouthpiece.

Round 1: *DING*

Just like with my first fight, stepping into the ring was no sweat. But the crowd was further away and quieter, which threw me off – made me tense.

I wasn't slipping well, and the few punches my opponent threw found their target more easily than I would have liked.

Another young guy, he was quick, and hit me with several easy 1-2 combos. Why I was just taking them, I don't know. But I eventually snapped out of the daze, and just as Jamey had suggested, my endurance was a weapon.

By the middle of the second round he was clearly winded. I was just getting warmed up.

He'd grimace, grunt and even moan when I'd land hard shots. It started to feel like I was picking on the younger brother I never had.

His expressions and sounds were more personal than I was used to. Fighters aren't supposed to groan and wince, though thinking back, I'd made exactly those noises and faces against Triston sparring. And just like Triston had hit me anyway, I hit this guy anyway. But it was weird.

Maybe I was too merciful to be a fighter. Maybe it was my old Jiu Jitsu instructor, Dr. Carter's, fault.

To stave off my punches and catch his breath, my opponent tried wrapping his arms around mine and leaning on me like you'll sometimes see the pros do. He'd apparently been well-coached. But I was pretty sure his squeezing was tiring him more than me, and so just let him.

Near the end of the second round, I had him backed into a corner and he tried his arm wrapping thing again. I made him pay by dipping down, freeing my arms, and delivering rapid shots to his ribs: *pow-pow-pow-pow-pow-pow-pow.* They weren't very hard, but the rapid succession made for a cool effect. I thought:

> "Now that's the Pac Man speed I've been practicing."

That felt good, and when the bell came at the end of the second round, I was beginning to believe I just might win this thing.

But then at the beginning of the third he landed a couple of early punches that caused the strap on my headgear to slip up over my chin. I tried to continue, but realized it wasn't going to work. I approached the ref, who sent me to my corner where Poke pulled the strap back down.

When the ref signaled for the action to resume, my opponent must have thought I was tired or injured and had faked a headgear malfunction so I could rest. This was not the case at all. When he charged forward I drove him back into the ropes where he was an easier target.

Though I had the strength and momentum, I was cautious. Like Ali playing "rope a dope" on Foreman, Triston would sometimes back into the ropes and lay a trap. I'd go in and hit him, he'd cover up, and once I'd worn myself out he'd bounce off the ropes, hook my face, and make me curse (though not out loud).

But this fighter had no such ploy in mind. I'd simply worn him down, and once backed up his offense was negligible, his defense failing.

I was beating him so badly the ref stepped between us and gave him a "standing eight count." This is where a boxer is receiving so much damage the referee stops the fight, sends the aggressor to a neutral corner and counts to eight so the hurt fighter can compose himself.

Following Andrew's programming tricks, I had actually visualized this. Seeing it come true was a great feeling. It wasn't a knockout, but when the referee intervenes, you know you're kicking butt.

While the ref was counting, Poke was behind me, yelling:

"You've worked hard for this, Matt. When it's time, *go get him.*"

I was itching to do just that, but right as the ref got to eight, dude spit out his mouthpiece. When a mouthpiece hits the mat, intentionally or not, the ref stops the action and takes it to the fighter's corner to be rinsed off. After that eight count I couldn't believe this guy was buying even more time. I was definitely smelling blood, and ready to finish the round in convincing fashion.

Poke yelled again – "*You've worked hard for this*" – and when the ref finally signaled for us to continue, I rushed in, covering my face with my forearms for what I thought might be a surprise blow (that didn't come), and continued my combinations, most of them straightforward, hard 1-2s, with a few left hooks mixed in.

That last round went by quickly – too quickly for a guy who was feeling great, facing a struggling opponent. He couldn't wait for the round to be over. I was wishing we had another two or three.

No surprise this time. The announcer read the decision and the ref lifted my hand in victory, a moment I'll never forget.

I came away from that fight knowing that my endurance was good, satisfied to have a clear win, and now eager to score a knockout. (I hadn't realized that was even an option.) My cardio had won the day, and the lesson I recorded in my notes afterwards was:

"Go faster and harder. You can last; they can't."

Back in the bleachers, I made small talk with an older couple sitting behind me. Turns out the gentleman was Orestes Salazar, coach of former Cuban boxing national champion and Olympic boxer Angel Espinoza.

Mr. Salazar had recently immigrated to Johnson City, and was just there checking out the fights. I asked if he had any tips for me.

"Work on bringing your hands up to catch punches. Otherwise, looking good."

I thanked him and gave him a business card. He'd call a year later, looking for help publishing a boxing book.

I also got congrats from teammates, as well as a few fans who had made the drive. One was a high school classmate named Robby whose mother, a teacher, had once saved me from my old nemesis, Larry.

Larry usually reserved his bullying for the school bus. But on this occasion he used the excuse of me splashing mud on his favorite shirt to pick a fight outside the school (in front of the old Home Economics Building, for fellow Vonore High alum).

Per usual, I backed down – refused to remove my backpack and apologized profusely rather than putting up my dukes.

Robby – or at least his mom, Darlene – had seen me at my most cowardly. It was nice having him there a quarter-century later to witness the opposite.

Watching the fight months later, there's a moment in the final round when I deliver a 1, 2, 3 (jab, cross, hook) combo that appears to momentarily knock my opponent out. If you find it online, fast forward to the 4:51 mark.

I've got him on the ropes, and when I throw that combo the kid, probably 19, goes limp and begins to fall face-first towards the canvas. About that time you can hear Jamey yell, *"He's hurt!"*

But I'm in the way, catch him on my forearm, he comes to, and I hit him some more.

If I had *any* idea there was knockout power in these fists, I would have been ready to step aside and allow the effects of that combo run their natural course.

But I'll take the standing eight count. I'll take the W. And I'll take the *almost* knockout, which admittedly looks more impressive in slow motion. What? Don't tell me you wouldn't watch your almost knockout in slow motion, too...

Boxing was loads of fun, and oh so primally satisfying. Hitting dudes in the face – there's something about it. But I'd proven what I intended to prove, and progressed as planned.

And so with a 1-1 record, it was time to transition to kickboxing.

# Part III

## Ogle's

# Chapter 9

# The Legend of James Ogle

"James Ogle once dislodged a sparring partner's tooth, handed it to a spectator, and kept fighting."

"In his younger days, Ogle would whoop a smart-mouth using only his feet."

My first job had been flipping burgers at the local Hardees'. Just up the road was Ogle's Martial Arts.

It had been on Hwy 411 by the A&W drive-in for as long as I could remember. And out front stood Ogle's Car Wash.

Rumor around the Hardees' grease pit was that hitting the wash/rinse/wax selector box with a hammer produced free, endless washes.

I liked to keep my green '75 Coupe Deville clean for cruising the Wal-Mart (a 1990s courting ritual popular among rural Appalachians), but lived on a dirt road.

Free car washes? On a fry cook's salary?

Not making the connection between "Ogles Car Wash" and "Ogle's Martial Arts," I kept a plumber's wrench under the driver's seat, and anytime Hoopty got dusty (which was every day), I'd pull in and spray him down. Such a sweet deal – too good for punk teenagers to pass up.

Then one day a coworker came in with a sad look.

"I tried the car wash trick."

"Really? Pretty cool, huh?"

"Yeah, it was going to be cool. I hit the selector thing with a hammer, it came on, then Karate Master Ogle jumped out from behind a bush."

Mr. Ogle hadn't missed the money. But he had noticed his selector boxes going bad, and decided to investigate.

He didn't dislodge any of my coworker's teeth. But he did call the law.

I promptly found a new place to wash Hoopty, and paid to keep him clean from then on.

When it came time to transition from boxing to MMA, I could have driven to Knoxville and trained at Josh Cate's gym like my combatives buddy Andrew. I knew from a visit it was a quality operation, Andrew had won both his MMA fights under Josh's tutelage, and Josh had actually given me some fighting tips via email.

But his gym was an hour away, and while Ogle's club was small, his karate students regularly won area tournaments. Plus, he had a couple of amateur MMA champions on staff.

Before I could train in the man's gym, I had to settle up. I took a confession and $50 and headed that way. I found Mr. Ogle in one of his car wash stalls straightening hoses.

I introduced myself, told him how I was a bit wild in my teenage years, and had stolen more than my share of car washes. I told him the Air Force had straightened me out (more or less), apologized, and offered the money.

He paused.

"It was brave of you to admit that to me. But you keep it. Confessing is payment enough. Besides, it wasn't the car washes that cost that much – it was the timing mechanism that would go bad from kids banging on it."

I figured I'd leave either $50 poorer or with a couple fewer teeth, so this was a welcome relief. My conscience clear, I started training at his gym Wednesdays.

Mr. Ogle would lead class occasionally, but his students and amateur MMA champions, Matt Tallent and Buck Yates, were the primary coaches. We did Jiu Jitsu, wrestling, conditioning and everything in between.

But Matt and Buck knew my plan: box, do a kickboxing bout, then an MMA match. This was a midlife crisis redemption adventure, not the beginning of a pro fight career.

They agreed that was cool, and endorsed my preferred method of attack – striking.

# Chapter 10

# Wolverine Colossus

I actually started training at Ogle's while I was still with MCBC, even before my first boxing fight. Jesse knew my MMA plan and was fine with it, and there was mutual respect between the gyms.

Mr. Ogle had been a boxer himself before branching into Isshinryu Karate, Jiu Jitsu and other arts, and hung a Rumble flyer on the dojo door to promote it.

The Monday after the Rumble I got a call from Buck.

"There's a kickboxing match being planned for late June in Dalton, Georgia. You in?"

"Sign me up."

I said, "sign me up." But here's what I was thinking:

*I know how to box, and don't have any trouble stepping into the ring with someone close to my own* weight and experience. But kickboxing? I've only been doing that in a quasi-serious way for a couple of months, and have only had my own set of shin guards for a week. I don't yet feel flexible, coordinated or balanced enough to go three hard, effective rounds using and defending both hands and feet. The challenge: to get myself to a point where I am ready... in 7 weeks.

By the way, I'm currently rocking a black eye courtesy of Jamey. I thought after my public speaking coaching he might take it easy on me during sparring. Nope.

He rocked me with a hook that landed square on my right cheek, leaving not only a mouse [lumpy bruise], but a cut. It's all good. I'd rather be reminded to slip my head (rather than doing the moving punching bag thing) by him sparring than by a stranger in a fight.

Buck also offered a fight to another Ogle's student, Mario. Mario had been with the gym for a couple of years, and had won his debut kickboxing match. He told Buck he was in for Dalton, but seemed lukewarm, wary about not knowing who his opponent would be.

Unlike the pros, and just like amateur boxing, first you agree to fight, then you find out who you're fighting. I didn't mind. I just wanted a match. It was several weeks before I found out who my kickboxing opponent would be: Logan Steele.

*Logan Steele?* Could there have been any more intimidating a kickboxer name?

Buck couldn't find video of him online, so I was left to imagine what this villainous mix of Wolverine and Colossus looked and fought like.

His coach reported a 0-0 kickboxing record just like mine, and that we were invited to meet somewhere between 132 and 137 pounds. Having just clocked in at 142 on the gym's scales, I advocated for 137.

At the end of class Buck and Matt said that we'd be going extra hard the next two weeks. They'd bring in heavier duty headgear, and invite me and Mario to go all out – to knock one another out if we could.

"That's what I'm here for. Get some headgear and let's do it."

# Chapter 11

# If It Had Been Him...

Rather than a ring, Ogle's had a large wrestling mat elevated on a 6" platform that took up most of the dojo. The wall on the left had tall mirrors, and the wall on the right had a window with a nice view of the car wash.

Mr. Ogle had set up a camcorder there to investigate what was happening to his timers. I wish someone had been recording *him* the first time he saw footage of teenagers banging on his equipment. Just don't tell him I said that...

About ten days from the Dalton fight, Matt and Buck decided it was time. They cleared the floor and instructed me and Mario to go 80 - 85%. This would be the test before the test.

With the disciplined diet and cardio of 4+ combat arts classes per week, I was naturally between 140 and 145 pounds. And since I'd soon be facing Logan Steele (ugh, that name...) at what I assumed would be 137, I was probably closer to 140.

Mario, who was expected to fight at 170, was probably 185. He had cut pre-fight weight before, and still had time to get it down for Dalton if he wanted. But it wouldn't be easy.

Despite my prior martial arts training, my weaknesses had always been wrestling and kicking, and I'd just been doing the kickboxing thing for a few months.

Mario, on the other hand, had apparently been practicing for years, and it showed. He could kick high and hard, reload with balance and do it again. He had the weight, height and strength advantage. He'd fought in, and won, a real kickboxing bout. But he wasn't as good a straight fist-to-fist boxer.

So my plan was to stay either too far away or too close for his feet to do much damage. My sweet spot would be just close enough to swap punches – needed to negate his kicking advantage and amplify my punching advantage.

We touched gloves and went at it.

84

My strategy was working. When he'd get in punching range, my combos were landing. He was covering his eyes and even closing them some when I'd hit him, which is a very bad idea. While a natural reflex, it's hard to defend, let alone return fire, when you can't see. You have to train them to stay open.

I also had better cardio and was expecting him to wear down, when I could really pounce, like against Orlando who'd become my moving punching bag in later rounds at MCBC. (Orlando's probably going to sucker punch me when he reads this... Love you, bro!)

Then two minutes into the first round, *bam, BAM.*

Mario swore it was a punch, but I know what fists feel like. He threw a jab, cross combo, followed by a left foot to my right eye and nose. His cross landed solid, and I paused for just a sec to regroup (and appreciate the quality blow) when his foot came crashing down.

"Hmm, nice shot... **POW.**"

It felt and sounded like a car wreck – crunch, white flash.

I was hurt, but Buck and Matt, who were coaching from the sidelines, couldn't tell.

I kept my hands up, kept fighting. Even though I didn't want to take another shot to the face *("Is my nose broken?")*, I couldn't help but press forward. As I learned, that's just my natural fighting style. Whatever happens, pursue and punch, pursue and punch.

Mario, being the compassionate teammate that he was, could see in my eyes that I was hurt, and backed off.

Matt, who was coaching me (Buck had Mario), thought Mario's backpedaling meant he was gassed, and started pushing me to finish him.

"Go! What are you waiting for – *go!*"

But Mario really wasn't punching back, and I didn't want to take another on the nose, so we more or less stalked each another for the rest of the round, a gentlemen's agreement to continue but not continue.

With the bell came the blood. First a drip, then a stream. First on my shirt, then on the floor.

Mr. Ogle would ask a few days later, "Are you the one who bled all over my gym?"

"Yes sir, I'm sorry about that. I tried to clean most of it up."

I was in the bathroom stuffing twisted paper towels up my nostrils when Buck came back.

"Hey man, you've got Mario all torn up. He's outside crying."

"Crying? What the heck for?"

"I don't know. Just go talk to him."

I found Mario outside, the A&W behind him, Ogle's formerly free car wash to his left.

"Mario, what's wrong?"

"You're my brother man, and look at what I did to you…"

The paper towel twisties were soaking red, and there were early signs both eyes would blacken. Nothing I said seemed to help. Mario would look up at my smashed face, shake his head, then go back to crying.

But I was giddy! This was even better than the cut Singh had given me in my first out-of-town sparring match. I had Buck take a picture. (Check it out at YearoftheFighter.org, but beware of spoilers...)

For Mario, not so much. Being on a fight team is a special brotherhood. You go hard. But as Mr. Ogle emphasized, you never want to injure a teammate. Strong, but compassionate – in fact, strong enough to *show* compassion – Mario was having a hard time forgiving himself.

I did my best to assure him that had I landed such a sweet kick on him, no tears would have been shed. I wouldn't have been happy he was wounded, but we both knew what we were getting into. As Poke liked to say, "This ain't patty cake. People get hurt."

Mario never seemed into his Dalton match, and seeing my gory face pushed him over the edge. He officially withdrew, which meant Buck had to make some awkward phone calls.

But he still had one fighter in. With my bout a little more than a week away, there was no turning back, cracked nose or not.

# Chapter 12

# Fight Week

There were no guilt-free jogs or movie date nights during my last two years of graduate school.

"Shouldn't you be working on me?" my dissertation would incessantly taunt.

I read productivity and goal accomplishment books for help, and found this three-word gem from David Schwartz's *The Magic of Thinking Big:* Action Cures Fear.

Action does cure fear, but not just any action – has to be something that gets you closer to overcoming the thing you dread.

The one action that eased dissertation anxiety was writing. Not planning to write or thinking about writing. But actually writing.

Now, deep into my Year of the Fighter, upcoming bouts cast the shadow, and the one action that eased the stress was training. Not planning to train or thinking about training. But actually training.

A hard run, workout on the boxing dummy, sparring session or class – these were the actions that cured fight anxiety. At least temporarily.

And so spare time, when I could find it, was spent training, usually at the expense of my wife Lisa and three kids. They were supportive of my midlife crisis fight run. But I could tell they were sad that it was demanding so much of my attention.

The Monday before my kickboxing match Buck told me he and Logan Steele's coach had agreed we'd fight at 135 rather than 137.

"Can you do it?"

"Yeah, I can do it."

Having dropped six pounds in a day for that Rumble matchup that wasn't to be, five pounds in a week was doable, especially since I could drive down Friday to weigh in, then rehydrate and eat before Saturday night.

Cutting that much weight that quickly before had left me drained, and I hadn't stayed that light –

I'd dipped down then bulked back up. I wanted to make sure I made weight, but wasn't sure of the strategy that would leave me strongest.

My nose still hadn't fully healed. It looked terrible and was sore to the touch. I was still training at MCBC, and told Jesse I was worried one solid punch might open the blood valve. He'd once fought four days through a broken nose at boxing nationals, and told me about this salve stuff that could stave off a bleed. But Mr. Ogle was against it.

"If your nose bleeds so bad they stop the fight, let them stop it. Better to do that than permanent damage."

I trusted Jesse, but would be wearing an Ogle's Martial Arts Fight Team shirt this time, so didn't look into the nose stuff further.

Mr. Ogle was turning out to be a pretty good guy. Tough but just – Monroe County's very own Chuck Norris.

That day he busted my Hardees' coworker stealing carwashes? He caught eleven other people. The same day. *Eleven.*

Did he have any of them arrested? Nope. The police knew he just wanted to scare them a little, and so would pretend they were going to jail, but inevitably allow them to reconcile – promise to work off their debt and never do it again.

Were I the local karate master, I'm pretty sure after I saw the fifth or sixth guy hit my selector box with a hammer, some hammers would have went where the sun don't shine. But that's the kind of man Mr. Ogle is. Similar to Dr. Carter, strong enough to exercise restraint. Strong enough to not only forgive my car wash thievery two decades later, but to forgive many guys on the spot.

It was nice getting coaching from him and the MMA team while I was boxing, and from the boxing team while I was kickboxing. Every teacher has a certain number of tips that will resonate with a particular student. The more masters you study under, the more wisdom you absorb.

Before my boxing match in Johnson City Mr. Ogle had given me his view on luck:

"I could tell you good luck, but I won't. If anyone tells you good luck, tell them no

92

thanks, and then punch them in the jaw. You don't win fights with luck. You win them with talent. You don't need or want luck."

Maybe he didn't tell me to punch luck-givers in the jaw... But that's how I recorded it in my journal, and it goes well with the legend.

"James Ogle would punch a luck-giver in the jaw... on Mondays, *the throat.*"

Buck had said something similar about heart:

"Heart doesn't win fights. I've seen lots of guys with heart get their asses kicked. You need skill, ability, stamina. That's what wins fights."

Stamina, I was building on my own. My skill and ability were growing courtesy of MCBC and Team Ogle.

I received much advice during my run. These tips stood out prior to Dalton.

1. Mr. Ogle: Don't lean back too much when kicking – doing so takes your hands out of the offensive game. Keep your torso in the fight.
2. Matt: When your opponent is protecting his

face, for goodness' sake, don't just keep punching his forearms – go to the body. One shot to the head, then straight to the body; back up top if he drops his hands.

3. Scott (another experienced Ogle's kickboxing student and unofficial coach): If you're overwhelmed by a charging opponent, switch your stance (orthodox to southpaw) as you compose yourself and "find" them. Stepping straight back in the same orientation (as I'd been guilty of) makes you an easy target.

4. Buck: If you catch a guy bent over covering his face, step in and give him a roundhouse right to the gut, hard. He'd do the same to you. (I think Buck and Triston would have gotten along famously...)

The whole gym wanted me to win, but I could tell Matt was especially invested. He hadn't coached much before, and I think wanted his student to succeed for both our sakes. But he also made a point to lighten the pressure:

"There's not a guy in this gym who's undefeated. Go out there and have fun."

94

I apparently was having fun, for I took the time to record something silly in my journal that week:

*I happened to be working on the porch shirtless today, glanced down and noticed my chest hair is longer and thicker, especially in the very middle. Maybe I've lost so much weight my skin is retracting to the center, bunching up my man fur? Or maybe all this fighting has unleashed my ultra-manliness.*

It was almost time to put that ultra-manliness to the test.

# Chapter 13

# Thirty Minutes into Georgia

Under USA Boxing rules, fighters have to wait until a few hours before their match to weigh in. But the International Kickboxing Federation would let you do it 24 hours in advance.

Most kickboxers and MMA fighters will schedule a fight ten or even fifteen pounds below what they naturally weigh. Then a couple of days before the weigh-in they'll starve themselves, sweat most of the water out of their body, weigh, then refuel and compete at their normal weight the next day.

Since some guys do this, there's pressure for everyone to do it. If you don't and your opponent does, it negates the whole weight class fairness thing.

So I gladly drove an hour and forty-five-minutes one way Friday (thirty minutes into Georgia) to take advantage.

I'd never been to Dalton, but knew I'd found Ben Kiker's studio by the parking lot marquee:

AMATEUR KICKBOXING SATURDAY NIGHT

The door unlocked, the lobby empty, I could hear country music and the whir of a vacuum down a hallway that opened into the main gym.

I walked on in, and in the center found what I was looking for – an elevated ring. It looked smaller than the boxing rings I was used to; smaller than the one in Knoxville, the one in Johnson City, and MCBC's.

I thought, "Yes – the smaller the space, the less likely kicks will be a factor."

Three rows of carefully placed folding chairs surrounded it. Heavy bags lined the wall straight ahead, mirrors the wall to the right, exercise machines the wall to the left, and mirrored glass the wall adjoining the double doors.

Vacuum lady, who I guessed was Mr. Kiker's wife, saw me eying the ring and came over. She said weigh-ins would be in about 45 minutes, and that I was welcome to make myself comfortable. But she could tell from my face what I really wanted.

"Yes, you can walk around the ring if you like."

As a speaker, anytime I have an important presentation I'll not only rehearse in front of stuffed animals, but visit the venue the day before. I'll stand behind the lectern and deliver my opening remarks, sometimes the entire talk, imagining an attentive audience smiling back.

I had done this the September before in New York. There had been a lady cleaning and setting up in that hotel ballroom near Times Square, albeit for a very different event. She didn't mind me rehearsing, either.

The ring's surface was a light red velour, surprisingly taut with a good grip. The ropes were thin like plastic cord or surgical tubing.

I walked around the ring, then side shuffled, then did a few advancing and evasion moves. I visualized attacking, cornering & pummeling Logan Steele, whatever this X-Man looked and fought like. I saw the referee raising my hand in victory.

I saw Lisa and two oldest kids smiling on the front row. They'd missed my boxing fights, but would make this one for sure.

Satisfied, I climbed down and sat in one of the folding chairs to reflect, taking a few notes in my wallet notepad.

> *Hear: country music, the hum of a vacuum, fans*

> *Smell: fruity air freshener (probably that carpet dust stuff)*

> *See: small ring, def no bigger than MCBC's – good for boxing*

I also noticed a yellow banner above the mirrored glass:

> "'I can do all things through Christ who strengthens me' Phil 4:13."

I appreciated the spiritual encouragement there, I appreciated it at MCBC, and I appreciated it at Ogle's (sometimes Mr. Ogle would lead a team prayer before or after class). But I wondered how combat sports enthusiasts could reconcile Christ's emphasis on love and compassion with beating people up.

The fighting part is probably just a way to lure in the lost.

"Think you're tough? Prove it against real fighters, not punks in the classroom or on the street."

You channel their aggression into a productive outlet (with rules, gloves, and a referee to make sure it's safe), give them a little structure and discipline, show a little care and understanding, and pretty soon they open up to the love thy neighbor stuff. I didn't pursue fighting to change my evil ways, but Jamey was proof the formula worked. Jesse, too.

Fighters started arriving, and we moved back to a locker room to weigh in. I beat my 135-pound goal by more than a pound, the least I could remember weighing since Air Force boot camp. Logan Steele hadn't shown up yet, and with a long drive ahead of me, I didn't stick around to meet him. We'd get acquainted soon enough.

Famished, in the car I chugged two Boost meal replacements and a couple of bottled waters, and drove to the nearest gas station for honey-roasted peanuts and crackers. My belly bulging but still ripped, I looked like a pregnant underwear model.

Making weight was an important part of the battle. At least I could relax about that. And I'd had the chance to feel out the ring and visualize victory. Time to get home, sleep, and confirm the final arrangements.

# Chapter 14

## Destiny in Dalton

June 18th, 2016

As we left Ogle's that morning, Matt grabbed the fight kit he and Scott had prepared: hand tape, Vaseline (a dab on each cheek to help the punches slide off), q-tips and gauze (should my nose open back up), and something I wasn't thrilled about – a white towel.

Matt insisted it was only a precaution. But maybe I'd shaken his confidence when I ate Mario's foot.

In any case, fighters can't entertain thoughts like that. The other guy's coach needed a white towel, not mine.

We made it just in time for the 1 o'clock fighters' meeting. Mr. Kiker went over the schedule and rules. Still unsure what Logan Steele looked like,

I eyed guys I thought might be in my weight class. A few looked too light. Most looked too heavy.

There were some tall skinny teenagers I thought might be him. None were worrisome. I'd fought (or at least sparred) bigger and tougher, and their baby faces implied a lack of heart, not that heart alone was enough.

The only fighter that gave me pause was this tattooed, shaved headed guy in his mid-20s wearing legit Muay Thai shorts – the kind with the baggy crotch that make high kicks easier. Everyone else looked like an amateur. This guy looked more like a pro.

"He looks mean, and like he knows what he's doing. So long as it's not him, I'll be fine," I thought.

Killing time afterwards, Matt and I discovered that Dalton is the carpet capital of the world... evidenced by the dozen or so carpet factories, and signs reading, "Dalton: *Carpet Capital of the World.*"

We sat on dirt bikes at the local motorsports dealer, and browsed the mall bookstore. Matt was recently engaged, so we talked about married life.

I shared how I'd embarrassed myself threatening that Florida drummer, which caused me to reflect on why, and set this crazy adventure in motion. He could empathize, but didn't strike me as someone who'd get that worked up over a silly football game, let alone put up with bullying.

Back at the gym with a couple of hours to spare, I leaned under a heavy bag and tried to nap. No luck.

Teammate Scott showed up. He'd driven down to lend coaching and moral support, and while I was resting my eyes had confirmed my fear. The tough guy with the tattoos and shaved head? Logan Steele.

*"Dammit."*

We went out to my car to eat. Scott and Matt tried to cheer me up.

"Don't worry about that guy – you got him."

With the small ring, we agreed I should use what we assumed would be a fist-on-fist advantage. It would be easier to close the distance, easier to stay in punching range (and out of kicking range), and easier to corner and beat on him.

Or so I had thought before I actually saw him. Now maybe that small ring would make it easier for him to corner and beat on me.

The parking lot began to fill as the sun went down. The crowd rolled in and the first fights started.

My wife Lisa showed up with my two oldest, Justin and Emily, all of them wearing big smiles. I'd made a point to not invite them to my first match in Knoxville – I was too nervous. And while I wanted them in Johnson City for fight #2, they'd gotten held up at a baseball game and just missed it.

I gave them hugs, thanked them for coming, and escorted them to their seats. I was proud that they could see me there, a real kickboxer. However it went down, here I was, living the dream. A roomful of people, all there to see these crazy fighters. At 39, this former scrawny bully victim was one of them.

I went with Scott to the locker room so he could tape my knuckles.

The gym was darker, and the atmosphere seedier than my boxing bouts. Along the walls in the shadows between the equipment lurked fighters hitting mits and heavy bags, grunting and otherwise warming up with their coaches.

With USA Boxing, youth development and safety were cultural themes. Here I got the impression fans wanted to see a fighter get hurt, never mind the scripture on the wall. There was less mercy in these fighters' faces. More bloodlust.

My turn was coming fast.

The dark gave me permission to get wild. I took off my shirt.

Just behind the crowd near the stairs into the ring, Matt on my left and Scott to my right, I started bobbing, then bouncing, then jumping.

Matt was worried the adrenaline dump would burn me out.

"Calm down... *calm down.*"

But the predator atmosphere had infected me, and I was ready to rock.

This guy wanted to kick my face like Mario had, except without Mario's remorse. That pissed me off.

As the announcer introduced us, the ref noticed my shin guards weren't taped, which required a last-minute wardrobe repair from Matt, giving me a moment to reflect. Mr. Ogle had told me at the end of class Wednesday:

"Don't let him hit you in the first 15 seconds. This will frustrate and demoralize your opponent."

Sound advice from a master. But waiting just wasn't my style. I'd learned that in the ring, and probably in life, my natural approach was to pursue a target head-on, and to beat on it early and often. Initiative and perseverance were my strengths. Elusiveness, trickery – not so much.

The lights were bright. The atmosphere electric. The bell rang and I met my destiny in Dalton.

Thanks to Jesse and Poke, the punches came naturally. I stalked and pounded per usual, only this time kicks were in the mix.

Logan threw a few at my head that could have been devastating, except Mario had taught me a hard lesson. This time I blocked or dodged them.

My go-to foot attack was a basic front snap/push kick. From my natural boxer stance, I'd pick up my left knee and extend the ball of my foot into his gut. Early on these were legit kicks. Later, as I tired, more like hard shoves.

I really expected these to wear him down. After all, they were landing where you get the wind knocked out of you – the breadbasket.

But Logan Steele's abs were living up to his name. He had better stamina than both of the boxers I'd fought. And he really knew what he was doing for a kickboxer with an 0-0 record.

At one point we crashed into one another and he instinctively put me in a Muay Thai clinch: his hands on the back of my head, elbows drawn together, pulling my face and sternum down for easy knee shots.

This would have been useful were we allowed to throw knees. But as Mr. Kiker had reiterated at the fighters' meeting, knees weren't allowed. Logan realized as much and released me, and I gave him some punches in the mouth for his trouble.

I was getting more tired than expected. Using my legs as offensive weapons and defensive shields was burning a lot of energy and oxygen. Despite months of training, I was at my physical limit.

At the same time, Logan was holding up better than I could have imagined. Especially with all my kicks to his gut.

And the kid could punch hard. *Real* hard.

He'd landed a string of solid headshots in rounds one and two that left me woozy.

Then at the beginning of round three came an attack I'd never faced: a "Superman" punch.

Logan reared back as if he was going to throw a roundhouse kick to my thigh, but instead lunged forward like the man of steel flying into Zod, transferring all his power through his knuckles, into my jaw.

I was rocked like never before. In a daze, a voice came to me:

*"Oh man, I'm about to get knocked out... But maybe that's a good thing – if I get knocked*

*out, I can finally rest... And I've never had that experience... Maybe it's cool?"*

This made some sense. I was tired – more tired than I'd ever been. Resting sounding lovely.

And I'd never been knocked out. Maybe it was a neat buzz... Why not?

While I was thinking this through, Logan backed off, surprisingly giving me some space. Maybe he could see how badly I was hurt and was worried I might keel over.

"Do I get in trouble if I kill this old man? He did sign a waiver, right?"

But before he could charge in and finish me, another voice – a louder voice from deeper inside – replied:

**"No!** *Hit that son of a bitch!* Keep pushing – *no stopping!"*

The momentum had been in his favor. I was hurt, exhausted, and thanks to some weak voice from the ether, considering giving up, expecting him to knock me unconscious any moment.

My weaker side was ready to welcome that fate. "You've earned a break... Maybe it's fun..." But my stronger side knew getting knocked unconscious would *not* be a cool experience – forget that. I'd worked hard for this. I only had one more round to go, and I knew I could do it.

Despite being near what I thought was my physical breaking point, despite having had the shit knocked out of me, I kept going, kept pushing, kept hitting. I persevered, and the mighty Logan Steele backed down.

Thank you, strong side, for not giving up. And kiss my ass, weak side. I hereby release you from my psyche. Kickboxer me has no use for your worthless whining.

I snapped back and continued to pursue and punch as I always did. Watching the fight tape, it's kinda funny. I'll push forward, hit him a few times, he'll deliver a hard cross or two – which in later rounds would rock me sideways. His fans will cheer, I'll re-orient, find him, pursue and hit him again.

A few years prior, my philosophy students had noticed that I look an awful lot like the bad terminator from Terminator 2 – the liquid metal cop guy who kept on coming, no matter what. Maybe Logan was wondering how this almost 40-year-old kept coming through all he threw at me, and in such a straightforward, persistent fashion.

"Is this guy a T-1000 or what?"

But I was thinking the same about him.

"How is he still not tired after all these gut kicks?"

It was a crowd-pleasing, rock 'em sock 'em battle. I'm proud of my performance. I'm proud of Logan's. Neither of us gave up. Until the final bell, it was bam, bam, bam, bam, bam, bam, bam action.

Having lost the judges' decision at the Knoxville Golden Gloves, I didn't know what to expect in Dalton. We'd both had our moments, but the fight had been pretty even. He was a better kicker, and simply wouldn't stop. But I was a better puncher, and just as relentless.

This wasn't his home gym, but it was his home state. And while he had a large, loud cheering section, I'd brought two coaches and three family members, my five-year-old daughter, Emily, being my most vocal supporter. (If you find the fight online, be prepared to hear a lot of *"You can do it, Daddy!")*

Simply making it through that instant of doubt and weakness, what I'd come to call my "Bloodsport Moment," I was content.

In my first fight, stepping through the ropes without fear was the victory. In my second fight, it was the actual win. In this fight, it was my strong side persevering when it would have been easy and understandable to settle for a nap.

The judges were taking longer than usual to reach a decision. Mr. Kiker went over to see what the holdup was. The ref finally emerged with the announcement.

A draw.

Matt and Scott thought I'd won, and couldn't understand how three judges scoring three rounds could result in a draw. Maybe one had me winning, the other had Logan winning, and the third had scored a tie?

They didn't think a tie was mathematically possible. But I didn't care.

Less than two years prior, this was all fantasy, something other men did. Now here I stood, at the center of a freaking kickboxing ring, in front of a crowd of maybe 150, sweaty and busted up, a mean-looking sweaty guy beside me that I'd busted up, thrilled to be living that dream.

I'd not only survived a near knockout, but fought back and held my own. The scary tattooed shaved head dude with the Muay Thai shorts? Turns out he really was that tough. But it also turns out that so was I.

I hobbled down out of the ring and thanked the judges for their time. In the locker room I finally got to smile and cut up with the infamous Mr. Steele.

I congratulated him and his coach, and we even took a picture together. In it you can see his abs scratched up from my toenails.

Logan's apparently drunk older brother came back. Five minutes ago he'd been yelling for Logan to finish me, and so was cautious around the perceived family enemy.

He was giving Logan a hard time for not doing an even better job, calling him a puss. I made a point to praise just how tough of an opponent Logan had been, and thought of his brother, "If anyone's a pussy in this room, it's you."

Here's my journal entry after getting home at 2:08 that night:

*Earlier tonight I fought a man 14 years my junior to a draw in my inaugural kickboxing match, in front of my wife, oldest son and daughter.*

*I was the most tired I've been in my life. Walking out of the ring I was thinking, "Steady – don't fall off the platform and embarrass yourself..." And about three minutes into the drive home I had to pull over and throw up. That was not the case after either of my boxing matches, though the very first one (with that crummy mouthpiece) was quite tiresome. Lessons:*

- *I can kick. I threw and landed a half dozen straight kicks in the first round, right in the breadbasket. Each time I heard Logan grunt, so I kept going back to the well (not that they slowed him down). I also landed a roundhouse to his body, which was nice, though it was a tentative, experimental kick that next time I'll throw with confidence.*

- *My leg kick blocks need work. I dodged half of what he threw, but ate the other half, and now my left leg is nice and sore. Ouch.*
- *I landed some good body shots, and it's a good thing. I'm sure I depleted him some, yet he still went toe to toe the whole fight.*
- *Kickboxing is more exhausting than boxing. Throwing, eating, and worrying about kicks in addition to punches takes the exertion to another level.*
- *I can take a punch. This dude hit hard. But even when his punches landed square, I kept on coming, in most cases replying with hard punches of my own.*

*Competing in a culminating MMA match is going to take a new level of dedication. It's going to take harder cardio training, toughening of my shins and sharpening of my kicks.*

*It's also going to take better tying together of hands and feet. That front kick works for me – I need to connect it to a hard cross and drill the combo into muscle memory.*

Last, the thought crossed my mind afterwards that maybe this should be the culminating event. I felt satisfied. Plus, my kids have suffered evenings without me for almost a year now. Their neglect is a constant worry.

So I'm going to reflect over the next few days and see if winning an MMA fight is truly important to me. If I'm going to give it a run, this is the time – it's not something that I'd want to come back to at 45 or 50. Had I dominated this guy tonight, that would have solidified my commitment. But it was a struggle. I triumphed, endured, and I'm very proud to have the awesome memories. But the cutting weight, constant training, and stress of the events has been quite a bit.

Will I finish my Year of the Fighter as originally planned? Or decide 1 boxing win, 1 boxing loss, and 1 kickboxing draw is enough to satisfy my 85-year-old self?

I'll wear this black eye, breathe through this bloody nose, and walk on this sore leg for a few days and figure it out.

# Part IV

## The Judge's Decision

# Chapter 15

# The Day After

Bacon, pancakes and eggs for breakfast. Steak, shrimp, loaded baked potato, salad, preceded by onion rings and nachos for lunch. Cookie dough for a snack, followed by soft shelled tacos and salsa for supper, followed by more cookie dough and strawberry frozen yogurt.

I shamefully ate a LOT of crap the day after my kickboxing match... a post-fight splurge.

Once my sweet tooth was content, I knew it was time to recommit.

A journal entry later that night:

*Knowing that my next fight will be my last is a good feeling. I can train with more happiness, I think, having three striking bouts under my belt, already familiar with Jiu Jitsu, and knowing that on the other side will be a less... intense life, with more relaxed exercise of my free time.*

*Who knows – maybe I'll look back on this run as the best time of my life. But having lived it for the past year, it's been pretty darn tough and stressful. Looking forward to chilling a bit as I move into my golden 40s :-)*

*But first, what got me here won't take me to the next level – I need to reflect, pick a date (thinking late October?), sketch a plan, and make this MMA match happen. Let's go.*

# Chapter 16

# The Curse of Will Smith

Have you seen Will Smith's *Concussion?* I watched it shortly after Dalton. It's the true story of Dr. Bennet Omalu.

He goes looking for evidence of Chronic Traumatic Encephalopathy or CTE in deceased NFL players' brains, and finds it. Even behind helmets, the repeated blows can have a devastating effect on cognition and personality that sometimes doesn't show up for years.

I'd thought off and on about how getting banged in the head probably wasn't good for my thinker, but had accepted the calculated risk. Plenty of boxers are lucid into old age (all whom I'd met, in fact), and I'd only be doing this for a year or so – at this point, just long enough to ramp up for my pinnacle MMA bout.

But there's a scene where Smith is sloshing a jar of peaches to demonstrate how the soft, gelatinous brain slams against the skull with every blow.

I thought, "That's what been happening to my brain every time I fight, every time I spar..."

Guilt about how I'd been neglecting my family was also mounting. I'd been training at least four evenings per week, and with pre-fight stress, even when I was able to see them I wasn't in the best of moods.

So I started thinking harder about whether to retire with one win, one loss, and one draw, or to tough it out and do the MMA match I'd planned.

Jesse and Poke were closing the boxing gym July and August for summer break. So even if I continued at Ogle's, I would at least have Tuesday and Thursday evenings with the fam.

On the other hand, even with a lighter schedule, continuing would put my brain health at additional risk. I not only wanted to be able to recognize my grandkids, but to keep learning, creating, to do more speaking and writing, to live other cool adventures – fighting was just one of many to come.

Maybe I could take another decade's worth of punches to the face and never know the difference. Jesse and Poke were sharp. But they'd done their boxing when they were closer to twenty than forty, and in any case were two isolated examples, still relatively young.

I already had a strong feeling of satisfaction and achievement. Retiring early would demonstrate an ability to analyze and modify plans when appropriate. And I could possibly transition to something like family karate. Martial arts *and* family time – a win-win?

My little girl would also soon be starting kindergarten. Emily wasn't as far along with her reading as was Justin when he started, and apart from her needing me in her corner, Noah, who was about a year and a half old, was at a formative stage.

I always found it hard to bond during the pooping, crying phase. But when babies turn into toddlers, they become interactive in ways dads can more easily appreciate. Noah could finally wrestle, or at least roll a ball back and forth in the kitchen floor. And when he didn't get enough Daddy playtime, we'd both miss it.

I imagined being 85 and looking at two pictures of myself. One version pushed on and did his MMA bout. The other called it quits in July after watching *Concussion.*

At first I thought 85-year-old me would be more proud of the version who pressed forward. But I realized I was assuming the additional months of head trauma hadn't messed up 85-year-old me's brain, Emily's schooling, or my relationship with Noah.

Or my relationship with Lisa, for that matter. She'd been unfailingly supportive, but I'd kinda been playing absentee dad with all the training. My Year of the Fighter had in many ways been her Year of the Single Mom.

The solution: I'd assess how much longer I'd need to train, and how many more head blows I'd have to suffer, and then decide. If I gave up boxing, I'd only be exposed to sparring twice per week at Ogle's.

On the other hand, the MMA bout itself would be in those tiny, barely-padded gloves (the gloves UFC announcer Joe Rogan likes to hype), and my opponent's feet wouldn't be padded at all. Depending on his strategy (some guys just want to grapple), shocks to my brain might be even more violent than usual.

But it would only be for three rounds max, and I could train to take him out in the first to minimize damage to us both. I'd soften him with the front gut kicks I'd landed on Logan, box his jaw, then do a takedown (maybe a favorite Judo throw, "Osoto Gari"), take his back and execute one of the "blood chokes" Dennis had taught me in his living room ("Rear Naked Choke" sounds kinkier than it is) or ground-and-pound (hold him down and punch his nose until he said, "uncle"). Solid plan.

Iron Mike once said, "Everybody has a plan until they get punched in the mouth." This is true... But it's better to have a plan than not, and this one at least looked good on paper.

In my journal I wrote:

*Decision: assuming I can do my MMA match as soon as October, press forward and make it so. You'll be more proud of yourself, you'll never have this chance again, and the risk of a few more months of combat arts causing non-negligible brain damage is small.*

I typed that in the morning, but wasn't as decided as it suggests. Over the course of the day I texted or emailed five people: my best friend since kindergarten, my best bud from the Air Force, my favorite cousin (also one of my best friends), a former boss who'd recently retired, and a former professor, dissertation committee member and mentor who'd also recently retired.

Air Force buddy Mike replied fast:

> "Just keep the sparring light contact and don't use headgear when you're training. Headgear is supposed to make it way worse according to the experts. Full body kicks, but nothing going to the head unless light."

Best friend David did as well:

> "Man, in all honesty, here's my take. You're a brilliant man with an amazing family. If you were trying to prove you're not a pussy, and can take a punch, you've done it. If you were trying to show that you have extreme willpower, you've done it. You've shown your

son that a black eye isn't the end of the world, and know what it feels like to beat some ass. Feel good about it."

And Cousin Mike a bit later in the day:

"Um, I would err on the side of caution. You have a family to consider. It wouldn't be an ideal situation if you ended up with a traumatic brain injury and Lisa had to wipe your ass for the next however long you burden her. You've had your experience and have proven your non-pussy status. The question you should ask yourself: Would going further prove you're a badass or a reckless moron?"

# Chapter 17

# Wednesday Night Class

I hadn't yet heard from Professor John or old boss Gary when it was time for Wednesday night MMA. I was confident they'd reply – just busy guys.

Class was cool. I'd earned the right to wear my Ogle's Fight Team t-shirt, and did so proudly. I was still sore, and so the guys took it easy on me.

We joked about all the carpet makers in Dalton, and about the "Dixie Pig," a bar-b-que joint Matt and I had passed on our drive down.

Near the end of class, Buck asked how I felt during the fight. I told him good, but ultimately ex-freaking-hausted – tired enough to pull over and puke on the way home.

He and Matt elaborated on how much more exhausting MMA matches are, with not only kicks, but wrestling, takedowns, and groundwork combined. From MMA sparring with the combatives crew, I knew this was true.

Then Matt said, "Maybe after two or three more kickboxing matches you'll be ready for an MMA fight."

I thought, "Two or three *more* kickboxing matches??"

The plan was to do ONE then a single culminating MMA fight. I had little interest in another kickboxing match, let alone two or three.

I got it though. I'd survived, but hadn't dominated. And I'd left so tired (and possibly concussed) that I had to pull over on the way home and puke.

A gym's reputation is based largely on the record of its fighters, and I'd brought Ogle's a draw, not a win. I needed to prove myself further before they could trust that I wouldn't embarrass the gym in a cage fight. Fair enough.

But this didn't change my goals or personal risk tolerance. Box a little, do one kickboxing match, one MMA bout, then I'm done – midlife crisis complete, childhood bully victim redeemed.

That was the plan. This was not the plan.

Matt and Buck also suggested the following Wednesday we'd travel to another gym in Knoxville to spar. Great.

So I'd need to do 2-3 additional kickboxing matches, with all the head trauma that would bring, plus spar twice a week leading up to those 2-3 additional bouts, and now apparently travel to other gyms for additional sparring. Wonderful.

At this point two of the five people I'd reached out to had said go ahead and retire. I'd proven myself.

That night I was still waiting to hear from philosophy professor John and former boss Gary when I decided to finally talk to Lisa. Maybe I should have talked to her first.

I explained my desires, my concerns and my options. Reluctantly, she admitted it was hard for her to watch my kickboxing match in person. She didn't like seeing me hit Logan, let alone him hit me.

But after reflecting she said she'd prefer to abstain from taking a side. Why? So she'd be insulated from any regret I might feel down the road, whichever way I went.

This was wise, but no surprise. Lisa's always supported my big decisions: to try college in my mid-20s, to switch majors from pre-med to philosophy, to do stand-up comedy, to temporarily move the family to D.C. for work, to pursue this crazy fight thing.

We both have our flaws. But I can never complain that my wife doesn't have my back. Doesn't hurt that she's gorgeous.

Back to the journal:

*As I await input from John and Gary, one thing is for sure – whether I abandon or stick with it, I'm a changed man, forever proud. The thought of giving up now makes me both sad and relieved; ashamed that I might not complete this awesome journey, but proud that I'm considering putting my long-term health and family first.*

I finally got a reply from old professor friend John on Thursday morning:

"I think you should retire early. Everything you value in life depends on your head. (Yeah, your wife and kids would probably stick by you if you were senile 10 years from now or really

134

depressed all the time or uncontrollably violent due to a brain injury. But the satisfaction you get from your present activities with them would no longer be available to you.) You should retire now. You've proved what you set out to prove to yourself. You've got nothing left to prove other than you can stick with a plan (and you've already proved that multiple times).

It's not a matter of 'toughing it out' – the human brain – unlike the woodpecker's – is simply not designed to absorb multiple blows. It's not that you're a wimp or soft, it's that you've got a human brain in a human skull and you value that highly. Maybe if you were single, childless and eking out a living doing brute manual labor. Maybe not even then.

There are lots of other things you can do if you relish the feeling of being in top-shape and surmounting difficult physical challenges. My $.02 worth. For my money, a brain injury is the worst possible injury and my worst 'nightmare diseases' are brain diseases – e.g., Alzheimer's. That's where my values lie.

John

P.S. – I'd also say, don't let your son(s) play football. They may need an excuse – peer pressure – and you'd kick your ass all around the block if they sustained a brain injury playing."

Then later a reply from retired boss Gary:

"I've given some serious thought to your dilemma. While not my choice, you have expressed a compelling set of reasons for pursuing the MMA match. I do think it makes a great deal of sense to forego the boxing while training and competing in October, before you retire.

I guess it's all about relative risk and your comfort level. In reality our daily choices always involve an element of risk whether we are consciously aware of them or not. Having a family with young children certainly adds another dimension of course."

Final tally:

> <u>Air Force Mike and Ex-Boss Gary</u>: continue, but limit the risks

> <u>Professor John, BFF Dave and Cousin Mike</u>: retire now – you've proven yourself

> <u>Wife Lisa</u>: I love and support you regardless

# Chapter 18

## The Decision

After much procrastination, I crafted an email to Matt, Buck and Scott. Before hitting send I caressed my Fight of the Night trophy from Knoxville (apparently Denzel and I had put on a good show), my winner's medal from Johnson City, and my wrist wraps from Dalton. I kept lots of souvenirs from my run, including the "athletic cup" from my kickboxing match, though Lisa insists it reside in a dresser drawer...

I listened to Noah and Emily playing outside my home office. I stepped into 85-year-old me's shoes one more time. I considered the brain thing plus the family thing, plus how the brain thing could later impact the family thing.

The family thing had actually been a worry for a while. Here's an entry from that March, reflecting on anticipation of what I thought was going to be my first boxing match:

The weekend before my first scheduled fight, I was in D.C. for an ethics conference. On the outside I was saying hi to friends in the ethics bowl community. But inside I was drawn to thoughts of the ring – pushups and shadowboxing in my hotel room Friday night, a run on the treadmill Saturday morning.

One night in the hotel I had a dream that I was boxing outdoors with huge gloves that might as well have been pillows. The hardest part was keeping the fluffy cushioning part in front of my fists, which were flailing all over. At the end I was surprised to be announced winner – neither of us had done much damage.

Back home, I got word that the guy I was supposed to fight hadn't been at practice all week, and that our match was cancelled. All that tunnel vision, all that stress, all that worry, for nothing. My next chance would be the following weekend.

That evening I hit my Spar Pro boxing dummy alone in a dark garage. My hands seemed too slow, stuck in quicksand. While my teammates at the gym had been improving, I was afraid my growth was plateauing. *Frustrated and exhausted, I sat on the concrete floor and shed a few tears.*

*It wasn't just the fight stress getting to me. My little girl, Emily, had gently expressed her sadness that I was training so much, clinging to me when I would leave for class, and cheering on weekends when I reminded her Daddy didn't have to go.*

*That Wednesday I felt pressure to go to an extra class at 5:30. It was for MCBC's "A team" (the gym's competitors), and since Jesse was volunteering his time I felt an obligation to attend, improve, and do my best to represent the club. But I was already committed to Ogle's MMA class from 6:30-8, and knew that if I did this extra boxing class beforehand I wouldn't get to see my kids at all.*

*When I got off work I was still undecided.*

*"It's only for one year," "Jesse will be expecting you" and "you'll be fighting in a matter of days – you need all the help you can get" weighed on the one side.*

*On the other, "your daughter will only be four years old once," "she'll be beginning kindergarten this fall and needs reassurance that her father is here for her," and "you say family is most important – a man who took this seriously wouldn't struggle with this decision – a better man might not be selfishly boxing in the first place."*

*That evening the good wolf (my stronger, better side) won, and that staying home was the correct decision became obvious as Emily and Justin bounced with laughter with me on our trampoline. Later we watched a little news together. Nancy Reagan had died, and the commentators reminisced the romance she shared with Ronald. This reminded me of how distracted I had become.*

So many evenings I'd left them, Emily doing a poor job hiding her sadness, Justin trying to distract himself with a book, and Noah crawling or stumbling around, saying "Dada?" as I snuck out the door. I'd just been suppressing the guilt, part of the calculated tradeoff.

The end of a dream, it was more bitter than sweet. But I knew it was the right decision, and figured I'd punch 85-year-old me in the gut if he disagreed.

"Like your healthy brain and happy kids? Good. Now shut up."

On July 11<sup>th</sup> I hit send on my retirement email. Matt, Buck and Scott were universally supportive. They'd relay the message to Mr. Ogle. I saw him a couple of weeks later at a basketball game. He understood.

It was eerie being a Monday without a combat arts class. But my kids affirmed the rightness of my decision as soon as I got off work.

We started on the trampoline, then explored coyote territory on our rocking horses. Then the kids played on the concrete pad in front of the garage while I straightened up, storing the boxing and kickboxing gear in a crate by the Muay Thai bag Andrew had given me.

The wrestling mats around it had scattered from a hard session, and I slid them back into place so the family bicycles could fit more neatly on the opposite side. I pushed the Spar Pro out of the way. I knew I'd break the equipment out again to stay in shape and recapture that tough guy feeling.

And now it wouldn't be pure fantasy. I'd been a real fighter, and no one could ever take that away.

After supper we played a yoga game on the Wii, Noah climbing all over me as I struggled into the plough, cow and cobra poses, followed by 45 minutes of *Just Dance.* Justin sang on the console's microphone, Emily grabbed her Frozen mic for backup vocals, and I danced like a fool, glad to be doing something physical and fun that didn't involve hurting anyone.

I should pitch an ad for that video game:

Coordinated family cardio without head trauma – *Matt "Midlife Crisis" approved!*

Lisa took Noah to bed, and just before hitting the hay the older two convinced me to play a little basketball, followed by a quick ride on our neighbor's four-wheeler.

We closed the evening by reading a book about an oak tree, and how it grew from a seed to a towering icon over the course of American history. Emily snuggled with Lisa, quietly sharing fears about beginning kindergarten.

We all tried to console her.

"You'll do great, Sweetheart."

And Justin whispered a reassurance that always warms my heart.

"I'm glad you're my dad."

I'm glad too, son. I'm glad too.

# Chapter 19

# Overtime

I don't compete anymore, but Monday evenings you'll find me at Monroe County Boxing Club getting my weekly combat sports fix. My kids are more into Jiu Jitsu and Scouts, but are usually at the boxing gym with me, jumping rope, shadowboxing, hitting the heavy bags, sweating alongside Dad.

Jesse got married, and his wife, Carrie, is now a trainer at the gym. She runs a plyometrics station by the speed bags that includes medicine ball twists, "mountain climbers," and core work with bowling pin-looking torture devices. She's good at humbling the tough guys, leading by example, usually without breaking a sweat.

Jamey backslid a bit and got into trouble. Rather than prison the judge sent him to Miracle Lake, a rustic Christian rehab in the sticks. He'd been there for me during my struggle, warming me up, rooting me on, helping me become something other than a moving punching bag. So I visited him a couple of times, sent him a copy of my public speaking book and M.J. Ryan's *This Year I Will.*

He's out now and doing better than ever. Recommitted to his kids, gainfully employed, and speaking more regularly about his journey, he cites his relationship with Jesus as the reason he's the good man and father he is today. Kaiden's happy for sure, as well as Jamey's daughter, Kendel – both great kids.

Last fall Jamey led his first Sunday School class. He credits my public speaking coaching for his success, but he's a natural. He's still kicking butt in the boxing ring, and recently found a sport that showcases his natural talent – 5k races.

I emailed Logan Steele to see if he was still fighting. Sure enough, he said he had been going "balls to the wall" for about a year, and was just coming off of a monthlong break.

I looked him up on YouTube to see if any footage of his recent fights might be available, and found him winning one in 2009.

*2009?!* I thought he was a kickboxing rookie when we met, not a seven-year veteran. Apparently not. Which is fine with me. Makes the draw and my Bloodsport Moment even cooler.

One Saturday after this book was first released, I paid a surprise visit to Larry. No, not to ambush him Mike Tyson-style, but to give him a copy and let him know I meant it when I wrote in chapter two that you can't judge a man for what he did as a boy.

He was cordial, even inviting me into his home. I declined – had to get Justin to a basketball game – but we shook hands and parted as men. I hope by now he's read and enjoyed *Year of the Fighter.* And if he's reading this slightly revised edition now, knows that I meant what I wrote inside his cover.

Facing Larry wasn't easy. Driving to his house, which I'd found via google after acquiring his phone number from his sister, I felt some of that school bus anxiety from my youth. But after what I'd been through, I was up to the task. It was like one of those time travel movie paradoxes: John Connor had to send Kyle Reese back in time to impregnate Sarah Connor who then births... *John Connor.* Larry had to bully me so twenty years later I would be compelled to do the crazy fight thing so I would then have the guts to… *face Larry.*

Reflecting afterwards, maybe I should have thanked him. Without all those years of harassment, I'm pretty sure I'd never have stepped in the ring, never sat on a stool and spat in a bucket between rounds (just like Rocky!), never known that at 38 I could *almost* knock a guy out, or hang with a seasoned kickboxer for three rounds at 39.

Ah, the memories. I didn't mention this before, but Justin and my nephew Sam were by my side at MCBC many nights, which made for irreplaceable family bonding time. The whole thing was life-completing in many ways. That little kid inside me – I got to become his hero. Doing it alongside family and new friends was icing on the cake.

If you have a childhood dream (or unfinished business) that you've been putting off, let's do something about it. We only get this one life. Let's make it one our 85-year-old selves can smile about.

# Part V

# The Lessons

# Chapter 20

# Life After Forty

I can report that the other side of 40 ain't all bad. With four decades under your belt, you've figured out a thing or two. For one, you have a clearer idea of how a lifespan unfolds.

When you're a kid, all the characters appear fixed. "Memaw was born old, right?"

Somewhere between childhood and midlife, you realize they were once kids, too. And you begin to see in them your own fate, which makes whatever life stage you're currently in more precious. It's only happening once – better enjoy it while you can.

At the same time, you also begin to realize, despite the show, how little humans actually understand.

When you're a kid, you assume the serious-faced adults have all the answers. Then you make it to twenty, and reason that the thirtysomethings must be hoarding the wisdom.

"Thirty-five. I bet that's when it comes..."

By the time you hit 40, you have to concede that we're all full of crap – bustling along as if our careers and mortgages really are that important, talking about politics and parenting and history as if we really know what Aleppo is or how Bitcoins work.

Surprise: everyone's faking it. Even the high-paid talking heads with Ivy League degrees. Even lawyers. Even me. We all have your same confusions, your same doubts. Some are just better at hiding it.

I say this so you know you're not alone – so you don't think, "Maybe this guy could pull off a cool, life-affirming adventure, but that's just beyond me."

Whatever. That I could do it is proof anyone can. You just need a mustard seed of courage. For that, reflect on how short our time here really is, and how our current life season will not last forever.

Despite our many half-understandings and confusions, one thing we do know for sure is that we are meant for more than a nine-to-five, consumerist existence. *Work, eat, sleep, repeat* is beneath us, even when interspersed with toys and vacations.

At the very least, we need and deserve side journeys that make living worthwhile. And if we don't *make* them happen, they're probably not gonna. As Ferris Bueller observed on his legendary day off:

> "Life moves pretty fast. If you don't stop and look around once in a while, you could miss it."

One life. One brief window to make each season count

Ready?

Here are some lessons from my Year of the Fighter that I think will help, beginning with the importance of being true to yourself.

# Chapter 21

# Authenticity

Did a particular adventure come to mind while you were reliving my Year of the Fighter? Something that would redeem your past, or make your 85-year-old self especially proud, or your current self especially happy?

Make sure it's aligned with the real you. That doesn't have to be the *current* you – stretching is good, improving is good. Just make sure your goal isn't a remnant of someone else's expectations. Only invest in a big goal that's authentic.

Your life and identity are unique. Tailor adventures of equal uniqueness.

If partway through it stops feeling right, you have my permission to change course. I discovered I didn't only aspire to become an ass-kicker, but was committed to being a strong family man, and highly valued my brain. (There's a zombie joke in here somewhere – just haven't found it.)

So when training got in the way of giving my daughter extra support as she began kindergarten, and when the risks of head trauma became too weighty to justify additional punishment, I retired early.

Despite my initial goal, upon serious reflection and consultation with trusted friends and mentors, I discovered that I valued my kids and long-term health more than an MMA match, especially with two boxing and one kickboxing bouts' worth of memories and redemption already.

I could have switched to another gym that would let me do an MMA fight immediately, or tried to sign up for a bout as a rogue fighter.

But I'd proven what I set out to prove, and respecting all aspects of my identity required conceding as much. As my cousin Mike put it (as only a good cousin can):

"Would going further prove you're a badass or a reckless moron?"

The decision to stop fighting turned out to be as tough as the decision to begin. But it was the right thing to do in light of my complex mix of values.

Childhood wuss me was vindicated. It was OK (and smart) to hang it up when I did.

You, too, are a complicated creature. As you pursue your own grand adventures, chart a course that honors that complexity. And don't be afraid to take detours that feel right. The authentic you may not reveal itself until well after an adventure is underway.

# Chapter 22

# The Formula

As you consider options that would make your life more vivid, memorable and worthwhile, add to the authenticity rule two criteria:

a) **It's a little scary**

b) **You'll be proud**

I've used these life adventure rules to earn a doctorate (I knew I'd be in my 30s when I finished, but figured I'd be in my 30s anyway – might as well have a Ph.D.), do stand-up comedy (was a weekend comedy club host during grad school – great fun), write (this is my third book), run a small business (between the Air Force and college I ran Deaton Asphalt Maintenance – sweaty stuff), and just used them to plan a summer family road trip out West.

I say *plan* a summer family road trip out West loosely. We've set aside two weeks to head towards Yellowstone and allow the adventure to unfold. With three young kids in a hatchback, wish us luck! Next year it's Europe, though Lisa doesn't know it yet...

It's a little scary, you imagine yourself being proud, it's consistent with the real you – go for it.

Modest stretch goals are OK. Don't worry that if you don't become champion of the world it won't be worth it. My doctorate is from the University of Tennessee, not Harvard. My comedy career was at Side Splitters in Knoxville, not The Laugh Factory in L.A. My fight record is 1-1-1, not 45-0.

Yet I still get to sign my name Ph.D. I still got the thrill of making live audiences laugh. And you better believe I'll be reminiscing my combat arts run at the nursing home.

This is for kicks, to make life more worth living. If you find fame and fortune, great. But the point is simply to enrich a life you can be happy with when it inevitably nears the end – a life worth talking about in heaven. Other books will show you how to land your dream career. Our aim here is to simply make our 85-year-old selves smile.

OK, have something in mind? Good. Here's my three-step "Success Simplified" formula:

1) **C**ommit
2) **B**egin
3) **R**esearch

162

Then of course execute, evaluate, persevere, etc. But those are the three basic steps: **C**ommit, **B**egin, **R**esearch.

To help make it stick, imagine yourself atop the Honda **CBR**900RR *Fireblade,* a crotch rocket as beastly and powerful as it sounds. Actually, there's no way I could hold up a 900, let alone ride it, so let's imagine their 600 cc model instead (falling over while trying to start a motorcycle was not the visual I intended to inspire).

Assuming we could learn to ride this thing, it sounds fun, right? Now imagine having similar fun living the dreams you've been putting off. **CBR**, baby – *the* path to excitement.

Know that I'm only simplifying what the success gurus preach already, and what's worked for me. The one possible twist is the order.

"Shouldn't **R**esearch come first?"

Nope. It's third for a reason.


## *Commit*

Step one is **C**ommitting to the goal, and you do that by writing it down.

There's something about putting pen to paper that transforms a someday, maybe *wish* into a concrete inevitability. Goals > Wishes

Achievement expert Brian Tracy insists handwriting as opposed to typing a goal better engages the subconscious mind. Whether that's true, I have found recognizing a goal in my own handwriting does make it more compelling, harder to ignore.

Fair warning, though, that handwriting a goal is also more intimidating. You're admitting what needs to be done, and committing to doing something about it. The "what if" worries will try to convince you to settle for things as they are.

"What if you commit to doing it? *You might fail.* Someone might find out! Let that dream remain a fantasy – you can't bear failure..."

Whatever. When you inevitably stumble, be proud for having the guts – it's just part of the process, as anyone who's achieved anything knows.

Michael Jordan talks about the hundreds of last-second shots he had to take, and miss, in order to hit the few dozen he did. Failure is a necessary part of the process. Accept that, and the potential of messing up loses its bite.

If you see someone striving and struggling, respect them for trying. Most people would rather live a life of quiet desperation than risk failure. It's not until their deathbed that they realize the real risk was having existed yet never truly lived. This is not you. Your life's end may still be regretful, but it won't be for lack of living.

Overcoming this early mental hurdle can be tougher than the actual journey. But know that the fear of commitment is normal, and that you don't need a treatise. Just grab a piece of scrap paper and sketch the basics: "earn pilot's license" or "open restaurant" or "acquire pet shark." Whatever.

Write it small and keep it to yourself if you want. When I first wrote, "Win an MMA fight before I turn 40," I didn't tell a soul for months. And there were months before then that I refused to write it down – too timid to embrace my own challenge. But it wouldn't go away, and when I finally went all in, it felt great.

After you commit that big goal to paper, sketch a few things you need to do to make it happen:

"schedule orientation flight" or "recruit chef" or "solicit shark smugglers on the dark web with Bitcoin."

Simply mustering the courage to write it down is a small but crucial victory. Then outlining the broad steps will reassure and set your subconscious mind in motion to work out the details.

And don't let the curse of perfectionism stand in your way. It's tempting to delay until you have a plan that's articulated perfectly or conditions are just right.

> "Maybe I should start a photography business... but I don't have a camera. No, I want to run a marathon... but my knees. No, that stand-up comedy thing sounded cool... I just can't decide!"

Don't get caught in the "paralysis by analysis" trap. Just pick something and get going. You'll figure it out.

### Begin

Once you've committed your goal to paper, **B**egin to take action, any action. Start the *doing* now.

Why is acting the second step rather than the third? Remember this three-word gem from David Schwartz: "Action Cures Fear."

Starting the habit of doing rather than wishing and wondering shifts you out of watcher, spectator, procrastinator mode and into achiever, doer, winner mode. It builds courage and momentum.

A big part of you would rather wait life out than try anything new. Newness involves risk, and what Seth Godin calls our "lizard brain" hates risk – it wants to keep everything safe and familiar, even when the safe and familiar is pathetic and sad.

But the real risk is finding yourself nearing the end of this life having never given it a true go. We only get one, and it will end. That should be motivation enough to do something cool with it. As Andy Dufresne said in Shawshank State Prison, "It's time to get busy living or get busy dying."

Delay action too long and your 85-year-old self will have nothing but dodged opportunities to lament. This is probably why so many old folks are depressed. There's the arthritis... But they also know they didn't live the life they were capable of. This is probably a big reason I was so grouchy at that football game, though the ten straight losses might have had something to do with it...

A favorite quote from General George S. Patton to help you get over the hump:

"A good plan violently executed today is better than a perfect plan executed next week."

It doesn't have to be perfect. It won't be perfect. Just get going.


## *Research*

As life coach Jim Rohn used to say, and his protégé Tony Robbins loves to repeat, "Success leaves clues." Once you've taken a few fear-curing, momentum-building actions, **R**esearch those clues.

Free blog articles and YouTube vids are a start. But real experts who've taken the time to craft something valuable expect compensation. So where's all the wisdom hidden?

*Books.* They forget to teach us in school that anything we'd like to do or become or accomplish, someone's written a good book on it.

A favorite during my fight run was Smokin' Joe Frazier's *Box Like the Pros.* Frazier refers to Muhammad Ali as "the Butterfly" throughout, which he earned the right to do at The Fight of the Century in 1971. Ali got his revenge in '74. But any man who not only beat The Greatest, but knocked him down, has some legit boxing advice to share.

Instruction on proper form, strategy, mindset – I was able to borrow a career's worth of pro tips without having to spend the time to become a pro myself. This didn't make me an instant success. But it did accelerate my growth and give me an advantage over fighters of similar experience. I didn't have to figure out the fight game on my own from scratch – Frazier had already mastered much of it for me, and was all too happy to trade his wisdom for $15.99.

Your how-to book by your Smokin' Joe Frazier is out there. The thing you want to do, need to do, *must* do – someone's done it. Let them show you how. Aspiring shark owners see Vasanth Simon's *Exotic Pets Guide: Leopard Gecko, Turtles, Sharks, and Silver Fox.* If there are books on acquiring and caring for pet sharks, there are books on your dream, too. Find them.

I'll even bet there are coaches or mentors within your network. Maybe not shark owners. But you know someone who knows someone who knows a pilot or restaurateur. Buy them coffee, see how they did it. (I recently bought a local author breakfast for precisely this reason.) Gift them the opportunity to help you – mentoring is a wonderful ego stroke.

That's the basic formula: **CBR**. Pick an authentic adventure that's a little scary, and something you envision being proud of yourself having accomplished. Then write it down, power through a few quick wins, and borrow the wisdom of people who've done it already.

For me, it had to be fighting. Not redeeming childhood me was a piece of unfinished business my 85-year-old self would have never forgiven. And I had to do it while I was still physically able.

For you? It'll take some reflection. If you're honest, you probably know the answer in your heart.

If it's a little scary, and especially if at the same time it makes you smile, those are hints.

# Chapter 23

# Debbie Downers

Pursuing your adventure will remind some how they've settled. Their rationalizations about how doing more is impossible, foolish, will begin to crumble.

Who will turn negative is hard to predict. But it will happen. Your success – your simply *trying* to succeed – will be perceived as a threat.

Do not be deterred. People will get used to the proactive, adventurous you. If they can't, better to have a few true friends as a doer than many fake friends as a bystander.

Remember how my dad used to show that black stallion, Pepper? He had lots of horse-showing friends when he started. Pats on the back and "good job" consolations were common when he was losing. But much of that goodwill stopped when he started collecting the blue ribbons.

I never got good enough at martial arts to make my teammates jealous. They were nothing but supportive, members of a loose brotherhood of people crazy enough to fight. But several non-fighter relationships were strained.

I remember a friend scoffing at how I'd cut weight for my boxing matches. Instead of, "Dang, I wish I had the discipline to do that – can you give me some tips?" it was, "What weight class are you fighting in, again?" with a smirk, implying I had to fight little dudes to compete.

Apparently when I'm in top fighting shape, my innards, bones and muscles weigh between 140 and 150 pounds. As boxers and kickboxers know, adding mass would have just slowed me down. Not that I could have bulked up much anyway, but while big muscles are pretty, they don't translate well into striking speed or endurance. Except for the heavyweights, you don't see many bulky combat sports competitors for this reason – strikers rely on fast-twitch muscles, which tend to be lean.

Whether my friend knew this, I don't think ignorance was the issue. I think the issue was either that he had his own old bully issues he was suppressing, or he'd rationalized sustained fitness is impossible after a certain age. It's not impossible. It just sucks.

You might have guessed my Bloodsport Moment was the toughest part of my midlife crisis run. Nope. That was over in an instant. Not even Mario's nose-busting kick was the worst, though it did prove the messiest.

*Life without chocolate or ice cream, Christmas without my mom's fudge or Mayfield's eggnog, Easter without Cadbury's Creme Eggs* – that was the toughest part. My only treats during my Year of the Fighter (with exceptions I can count on one hand) were protein shakes. Jesse was even against Gatorade.

At the end of my first fight the ref handed me a long-sleeved t-shirt and a coupon for a hotdog and a coke. I thought, "A hotdog and a coke? Is this a cruel joke?"

I gave the hotdog slip to teammate Brayden (his teenage metabolism could better handle it) and convinced the concessions people a bottled water was more fitting. It's not that I don't like hotdogs. They're just not part of an athlete's diet, especially when he's pushing 40.

So I know better than most the pain of an ultra-strict diet. Me dropping and keeping that much weight off through sheer willpower exposed whatever story my friend had been telling himself.

Realizing what I assumed were his understandable motives, I was able to forgive his lack of support. But at the same time, many people were complimentary and encouraging.

My old Air Force buddy, Mike, wrestled in high school, and would periodically text to congratulate me for having the guts and perseverance to pursue my dream.

Combatives buddy Andrew, who'd been a fighter himself, gave me an old Muay Thai bag and let me borrow fighting mindset books.

One night I was coaching Gabe, a 7-year-old at the boxing gym, on his footwork. He thanked me, adding:

"You're one of the best boxers in here."

Why a 7-year-old's opinion would boost my ego so much, I'm not sure. But that comment made my day.

Folks at work cheered me on, despite me showing up to video conferences with black eyes. I learned the Tyler Durden mantra (you've seen *Fight Club,* right?):

> "Yes, these are bruises from fighting. Yes, I'm comfortable with that. I am enlightened."

People at church didn't know what to think. From a Sunday journal entry:

> *With two shiners, I got weird looks during and after this morning's service. The pastor seemed to look and preach directly at me (even more than usual). Maybe I should tell him I got these black eyes in a sanctioned bout rather than a bar fight.*

Maybe they were judging, or maybe they were just worried. Sometimes people will try to hold you back, not out of jealousy or insecurity, but love. The effect is the same. But they want you to play it safe, not because your success is a threat, but for your own good.

Here's a journal entry from April, 2016:

> *Last night I played Mom a clip of one of my sparring sessions. She commented on my weight – said I was losing too much. I told her I was hovering around 140 since that's the weight I plan to fight at.*

*She reminded me how I wanted to try football my senior year, how little I was, and how she just knew those big boys would hurt me. She said I came home with all this gear, went to spring practice, found out how rough it was, and quit. "You can't try to be a horse if you're a pony," she told me.*

*This was of course discouraging, and wasn't the first time. When I started training in martial arts in 2001 she shared some sage wisdom from an old riding partner: "You have to ride the horse you came on," meaning that I ought not do anything too dangerous, lest I harm my fragile little self.*

*So when she made the pony trying to be a horse comment I asked, "Well, did I look like a pony in that fight you just watched?"*

*"Well, no – I guess that wasn't the best analogy for the point I was trying to make."*

I think it clearly captured the point she was trying to make, which no doubt came from a place of love. I was sporting a fading black eye at the time, and I can't blame a mom for worrying about and trying to protect her boy.

This got me down for most of the rest of the night. But I was able to smile when I remembered how she used to coach me when I was a kid.

Anytime I'd get discouraged (over anything that didn't involve football or fighting), she'd remind me of the time I was invited to a roller rink birthday party, didn't know how to skate, and so I hit the driveway – literally – until I figured it out. I wasn't the most graceful skater at the party, but I was among the fastest. She never let me forget that I could conquer anything I put my mind to.

Parents cautioning their kids is nothing new. I'm guilty of the same. I knew I'd never be Mike Tyson. But I decided I'd much rather be the best fighter I could be than no fighter at all. My 85-year-old self insisted. So no worries, Mom.

Plus, maybe I was oversensitive. An uncle had recently told me at a reunion:

"Your dad tells me you're boxing. I told him I thought you were intelligent."

This same uncle was proud when I published my first book, asking for extra copies to take back to St. Louis. I doubt he knew anyone in need of public speaking coaching. He was just proud of his nephew, which was flattering, even in my 30s.

But he was an Army vet, a former military policeman, a tough guy. Why was he less excited about my boxing than my writing? I found a quote in one of the mindset books Andrew had lent me that helped:

> "I give back to others the responsibility for their own opinions and judgements."

Whether my ambition was threatening or worrisome, it didn't matter. Other people's opinions were their business. I was doing this for me.

You'll have Debbie Downers as well. Understand that their discouragement says more about them than it is does about you, and just keep doing your thing.

And don't think too harshly of them. Every parent knows how tough it is balancing love with discipline, guidance with encouragement, role modeling with freedom. So cut your folks some slack. They're doing their best. Friends and uncles, too.

And if you rode in on a pony, do not settle. Work him into a stallion – upgrading is allowed. Just ask that kid I *almost* knocked out in Johnson City.

# Chapter 24

# The Two Wolves

You can and should limit your exposure to Debbie Downers. But there's an inner critic whom we can never completely avoid.

I mentioned before that like most boys who grew up in the 80s, I'm a Rocky fan. Here's the champ showing Apollo Creed's son, Adonis, how to properly shadowbox using a mirror:

> "You see this guy here staring back at you? That's your toughest opponent. Every time you get into the ring, that's who you're going against. I believe that in boxing, and I do believe that in life."

He's right. At least partly.

You may have heard the legend of the two wolves. Stalking a deer, an Indian chief teaches his grandson:

> "Inside the hearts of all men are two wolves – one good, one bad. The good wolf is brave,

patient, powerful. The bad wolf is cowardly, fickle, weak. The two are in constant battle for our souls. You can feel them fighting in your chest: *thump-thump, thump-thump.*"

"Grandfather, I've felt the wolves struggle – both physically in my chest, and emotionally in my heart. But which is stronger? Which will win the battle for my soul?"

*"The one you feed."*

If your challenge is worthy, you will experience setbacks. If you indulge in self-doubt – if you feed your bad wolf – he will grow stronger, louder.

In the shower after a frustrating and painful MMA workout at Ogle's, wallowing in bad wolf self-pity, I had the thought:

"Well, I'm flying to D.C. next week for work – maybe I'll die and won't have to fight anymore..."

You know your bad wolf is well fed when you start thinking *dying* might be a welcome relief.

I had to remind myself of my reasons, of what formerly homeless motivational speaker Eric Thomas calls my "why," and recommit. Know exactly why you're pursuing your challenge, for your personal "why" is bad wolf poison. It's the one and only thing you're allowed to feed him.

A week from my kickboxing match in Dalton, I was sporting double black eyes and a sore (possibly fractured) nose, which made mustering confidence even more difficult than usual. I found myself lying on my garage floor questioning my sanity and dedication. The bad wolf wasn't whispering this evening. He was loud and clear.

> "This is ridiculous – you're not tough enough for this."

> "You're not a fighter and everyone knows it."

But my good wolf knew my *why:*

> "You only get one life – *one.* You've come this far; what are you going to do, bow out because your nose got busted? No – you're conquering combat sports now. It's now or never, and never is simply not an option. You respect yourself too much to back down. Get up and hit that heavy bag with the ferocity needed to get ready for your next fight."

Thank you, good wolf, for winning that day. That "only one life to live, it's now or never" *why* got my sweaty middle-aged butt off the garage floor when nothing else could.

Know your why. Use it. For you have an ever-present enemy.

During my Bloodsport Moment one voice said, *"sssssubmitttt... ressssssst..."*

Another yelled, ***"Hit him!"***

In the moment, my good wolf was louder. But the Sunday afterwards, that slithering Voldemort got his revenge, even convincing me to extend the splurge into Monday: raw cookie dough, ice cream, Reese's Cups, Hershey's (with almonds – mmmmm), York Peppermint Patties.

I rationalized that I "deserved" to "reward" myself. I wanted to let loose and enjoy, especially since I expected to soon be training again, this time for my pinnacle MMA match.

One version of ourselves is lazy, scared, apathetic. Another is ambitious, courageous, inspired. Eating all that junk was my lessor self getting back at my greater self. It was self-destructive internal revenge.

As you nourish your good wolf with bold, decisive action, with affirmations and positive self-coaching, your bad wolf may grow hungry, but he never dies. Always lurking, he'll tempt you to swap one unhealthy distraction for another, to put off your adventure until tomorrow, next year, to "reward" yourself in ways you know are truly punishment.

Freud called this self-destructive impulse the death drive. Steven Pressfield calls it "Resistance." And it's been said the greatest trick the devil ever played was convincing the world he didn't exist.

Bad wolf, death drive, Resistance, satan – whatever name you prefer, know it's there, and meet it with your eyes wide open. For it takes steely vigilance to overcome.

Patient, it waits for your moment of weakness: *"Let him knock you out; you've done enough; you deserve to reeeeessssssstttt…"*

Re-harden your resolve daily. The struggle within is winnable. But the bad wolf is strong, resilient. Some days he will win. The key is to not let one slip-up usher in a complete wolf reversal.

Though I'm great at it now, I struggled when I first started teaching. My lecture might fall flat, or discussion fizzle. Since I enjoyed his classes and he'd been teaching for decades, I asked my old professor friend, John, for advice.

"Don't worry about it. It's OK to have a bad class. Every teacher has bad classes. The trick is to not have two in a row."

You'll have bad classes, too. And that's OK. The faster you can mentally move past them (and cut your bad wolf's food supply) and focus on doing better next time (shoveling steak in your good wolf's direction), the more likely a string of victories is ahead.

I've used this trick to bounce back in the classroom, after losing my temper with my kids, after a frustrating sparring session, after getting off track from my workout regimen and diet – after *temporarily* failing in countless ways. It'll work for you, too.

Our bad wolf may be ever-present. But so is our good wolf. He remains poised to kick our bad wolf's ass – Mike Tyson rip-his-fur-off-in-the-street-bully-revenge-style (not that an ethics professor should endorse such violence...). All we have to do is feed him.

# Chapter 25

# Self-Coaching

In addition to writing your adventure down and sketching a basic plan, consider keeping a journal, as well as an affirmations notebook. Your good wolf thrives on self-coaching – think of every affirmation as a good wolf Scooby Snack.

On Andrew's advice, in my notebook I'd handwrite things like:

> "I am a battle beast... I love hardcore battle training... Exhaustion is simply a barrier to push through... My body *will* respond when I need it."

I know it sounds silly. "Battle beast?"

But training often sucked, and I didn't initially view myself as a fighter. I needed to step into the me I wanted to become (fearless, capable), and making that vision a reality was easier when I said and wrote the things *that* version of me could honestly say and write.

The self-coaching really helps. Sometimes it's the only positive reinforcement you're going to get. Not because no one else cares. But because a) everyone's busy with their own lives, and b) no one understands your challenges and dreams like you.

Repeating affirmations also helps bring the desired you into existence. You begin to accept that you really *are* a battle beast, that you really *do* love hardcore battle training.

Part of the point is to self-create that new, enriched you. My experience in the ring didn't just add a line to my life resume. It added perspective, confidence, knowledge, character. As you progress through your adventure, how you approach new challenges, and even day-to-day life, will be forever different, improved.

So choose adventures that you'll not only be proud of and that are a little scary, but that you envision molding your character in a direction you endorse. We can't choose our genes, the families or communities into which we're born. But we can envision the sort of person we want to be, and bring it about via our thoughts and actions.

Go ahead and visualize the person you aspire to become. What are the core features of their character and abilities? Write and say those statements in the first person:

> "I am a confident, competent pilot. I look forward to opportunities to fly more and improve my skill. I have studied, practiced, and can calmly negotiate all obstacles that may arise in the air."

Whatever it is, hold your head high when you say it. This isn't make believe. Speak your vision into reality by first accepting it yourself.

The Neurolinguistics Programming experts recommend doing this right before bed and first thing in the morning, when our minds are most malleable and open to suggestion.

And also consider keeping that journal. Putting your thoughts on paper will help you make sense of them, and more deeply appreciate the journey. Plus, progress begets progress. Recording it will remind you of all you're accomplishing and help keep you on track.

If you catch yourself debating *when* would be the perfect time to tackle the first or next step, that's the wrong question.

There is no perfect time. If something is important, you make time, and you begin it sooner rather than later. Awaiting perfect circumstances is just another bad wolf ploy.

I remember my bad wolf convincing me to keep Scott at a distance during a sparring session at Ogle's. He'd invited me to work on punch/kick combos inside, and was interested in coaching and teaching, not winning or dominating.

But Scott's a big dude, probably seventy pounds heavier and four inches taller. (He and Matt flank me in a post-Dalton picture at YearoftheFighter.org.) It was one thing to think, "I'm not afraid; charge in there and throw with him – *now.*" It was another to do it.

I hesitated, kept my distance, and rationalized I'd figure out kickboxing combos another night.

I remember similar hesitance my senior year. Of my forty or so classmates, most were either too busy, too broke, or just weren't interested in a coordinated trip to the beach. So I jumped in my buddy Richie's lowrider truck and headed to Pigeon Forge, a tourist town at the base of the Great Smoky Mountains.

We hit an arcade and a go kart track, but the reason we went was to bungee jump, something new in Tennessee in 1995. Once strapped in and at the top of the platform, I must have stalled for thirty minutes.

"Do you have a family? Where did you go for your senior trip? What time do you close?"

I'm surprised the attendant didn't just push me off.

What I learned, forgot, and had to relearn, was that once you've made up your mind, jump. If I'd known how awesome the fall and recoil bounces were going to be (*wheee!*), there would have been no waiting.

People who wait for the perfect time to get married or start a business or begin college (or become a fighter) wait until they're dead. This is not you.

You know what you need to do. You know the formula. If you haven't already, go ahead – commit, write it down.

Here's a good spot:

# Chapter 26

# Matrix Moments

Pursuing cool adventures consistent with the authentic you will make for a more fulfilling, worthwhile life. But if you're not careful, it can still feel hollow.

Philosophy professor Kieran Setiya warns in *Midlife: A Philosophical Guide* how chasing goals can actually lead to dissatisfaction and frustration, even when you achieve them. For once a goal is accomplished, that's it. You make your first million bucks or buy a Corvette or crest Everest. Now what?

You've earned bragging rights. But that seems a weak consolation after all the buildup. One fleeting moment to relish the victory, then... on to the next goal?

During my Year of the Fighter I had one big end goal in mind – to compete in (and ideally win) an MMA bout before 40. I never fought that MMA match. But I did box twice and kickbox once, which was super cool, more than satisfying my original "why".

Was the accomplishment buzz I felt after each hurdle – first sparring session, first fight, first kickboxing bout – fleeting? Was I left empty and in need of another goal to pursue?

Not at all. The reason is that I was following Setiya's advice without even knowing it.

In his book, which I read after my run, he recommends we tackle big goals as we might a hike or a bike ride or anything we do simply for the pleasure of doing it.

A hike's success isn't measured by the miles you walk or the number of deer you count, but the enjoyment you experience during. Dancers dance for the joy of dancing. Fishers fish for the serenity of fishing.

As you work to earn that degree, open that restaurant, or run that half-marathon, relish the process. Appreciate the small victories that happen in the moment, and the coolness of simply being on the path.

There were many times during my combat arts run I paused and thought:

"I'm really doing this. I'm not a spectator. These people are here to see *me* fight. Cool!"

Don't wait until your adventure is complete to give yourself permission to enjoy it. Embrace and celebrate the process.

That process isn't always fun. It will at times be tough and scary. But know the more you put into it, the better you'll get and the less scary it will be. From my fight journal:

*Watching a UFC rerun last night, for the first time fighting looked like fun. For years, it looked stressful and scary. Today, for the first time in my life, it just looked like fun.*

There's an old saying: "Do the thing you fear most, and the death of fear is certain." Fear dissolves in the face of experience. I want you to have growth revelations like these:

*Sparring tonight, Kaiden landed a hard right to my temple, which produced the pretty white flashes (\*\*oooohhhh, pretty white flashes\*\*). I registered the shot, pressed forward, and within a few seconds was fine. The more you survive, the more you realize hard shots are absorbable – it's just a matter of experience.*

Plus, you get to have *Matrix Moments.* Remember the scene where Morpheus and Neo go into the sparring simulator to practice Kung Fu? (If you don't, Netflix *The Matrix* tonight – a sci fi favorite.)

Neo's trying to hit Morpheus, but doesn't believe in himself. Then Morpheus tells him, "Stop *trying* to hit me and hit me!" which spurs a breakthrough. Suddenly Neo's fists are so fast they're a blur, and he's able to calmly defend Morpheus's strikes with one hand behind his back.

Breakthroughs aren't just for the movies. We can have them in real life.

*Tuesday I had my first "Matrix Moment." I was sparring a guy about 25 pounds heavier who was keeping me at distance, landing more shots on me than I was on him. At the end of the first round Jesse gave me the option to let another fighter take my place.*

*I refused, Jesse laughed (acknowledging my determination), and about 30 seconds into the 2nd round I charged in to close the distance, dude backed up near the ropes and stopped, and we went at it for maybe 10 seconds.*

*10 seconds doesn't sound like a long time, but we must have thrown two dozen punches apiece.*

*I've been involved in cool exchanges, but this was the first time I was going really fast with both my offensive hands and my defensive body. I surprisingly kept my eyes open and on his head the whole time (before I'd usually look at my opponent's chest or even the ground). For a few seconds I felt like Neo realizing just how fast he could be.*

Notice how this didn't happen in an actual fight, but while training. I had some awesome moments during my fights, too. But opportunities for epiphanic growth can occur anytime we're stretching, pushing.

I want this for you. An expanding comfort zone is a beautiful thing. Your own Matrix Moments are waiting. Let's go get 'em.

# Chapter 27

## Carpe the Season

Imagining what my 85-year-old self would think was enough to get me off the couch and into the ring. Nearing 40, I knew it was then or never.

I planned to stay in shape long past middle age. But at 45, Logan's Superman punch might have knocked me out cold. At 50, I might not have made it past Triston.

Life offers experiential opportunities in seasons like that. There are cool things you can only do when you're a kid, only when you're a teenager, only when you're still strong enough to take an angry 20-something's punches to the jaw.

If you wait until you're 30 to ask the homecoming queen on a date, she'd better be the queen from back-in-the-day, not the current, reigning queen. You can play hide and seek with your kids when they're 20. But I'm told it's less awkward when they're 8. Whatever season you're in, do the cool things you've always wanted to do before it passes.

If you're nearing midlife, the good news is that you're probably still healthy enough for most athletic stuff, young enough to go back to school and change careers, and at the same time old enough to have the resources and credibility to get what you want.

We gain a natural authority as we age. Unless you have a neck tattoo, the police assume you're law-abiding. Greying hair in many ways sucks. But becoming a "sir" or "ma'am" has its advantages – people tend to give you the benefit of the doubt.

Regardless of whether you enjoy the benefits of youth, midlife or seniority, carpe your season. That is, *seize* your season.

I'm of course channeling the late, great Robin Williams in *Dead Poets Society*. The long-dead men in that black-and-white photo he shows his students – they hauntingly whisper "carpe the season" to us, too.

Realize what cool opportunities are available now that won't be later, and take that plunge.

Ethicist Rosalind Hursthouse once said we're in "the happy position of there being more worthwhile things to do than can be fitted into one lifetime." I'm glad we have options. But man, wouldn't it be nice if that lifetime were a little longer?

The good news is that our limited time forces us to choose wisely, and that we actually have enough time to choose *widely* as well.

Some will tell you the key to success is to focus exclusively on one thing. You don't become Muhammad Ali dabbling. But while Ali boxed to the exclusion of most everything else, consider Leonardo da Vinci – a master of art, engineering, architecture and invention.

I'd rather enjoy dozens of life's glorious options in depth than one option all the way down. You're free to disagree. But for my time, adventures (plural) are where it's at.

The paths you choose are your call. But please do go ahead and choose. 85 will be here before you know it. And I want you to be able to experience and relive your own epiphanic joys:

> "Ah, so *this* is what being a comedian is like, *this* is what being a professor is like, *this* is what being a fighter is like."

Each of these started as a wish, a hope, a dream. But dreams are for suckers. We translate our dreams into goals and get on with it.

**C**ommit, **B**egin, **R**esearch. No one's going to hand you the adventure you want and deserve. You have to take it.

I'll leave you with one final journal entry from the day after my first fight:

> *I went to sleep last night with a huge smile on my face, and when thanking Jesse this morning, told him that even if I was paralyzed*

*tomorrow and could never box again, I'd die satisfied that I conquered my fear and did it.*

*There's a 10-year-old bully victim deep inside that's really happy right now, despite how the judges scored the match.*

*Being a fighter feels damn good :-) 99% of men fantasize about it. Only a fraction actually do it. I'll go to my grave proud that I'm a member of that percentage of a percent.*

# If You Liked It...

My readers are my marketing department, so if you enjoyed *Year of the Fighter,* consider telling a friend or writing a review at Amazon.

If you happen to use it to tackle your own cool adventures (I hope you will), shoot me an email – I'd love to hear about them (I'm easy to find online).

And I would tell you good luck, but you know what Mr. Ogle says about luck-givers...

Thanks for reading,
Matt

For fight footage, pics of the Monroe County Boxing Club team and Ogle's crew, and a little bonus inspiration, visit

# *YearoftheFighter.org*

# Additional Titles by Matt Deaton

## *Ethics in a Nutshell: The Philosopher's Approach to Morality in 100 Pages*

Yes, the crazy midlife crisis fighter guy and (former) carwash thief really is a (part-time) ethics professor.

*Ethics in a Nutshell* is primarily for college ethics students and ethics bowl competitors (learn more about ethics bowls at a blog I run: EthicsBowl.org), but at 100 pages, it's written to be accessible to anyone with an interest.

To see if you might like it, check out mini-lectures on each chapter and an "Ask Matt" interface at EthicsinaNutshell.org.

## The Best Public Speaking Book

Considering an adventure that will include public speaking? Here's how to do it comfortably and competently, from conquering nervousness through message delivery.

If you don't have time to read it, just follow my Three Commandments: Know Thy Material, Be Thyself, and Practice.

But if you do have time, I bet you'll enjoy the "Urban Honey Badger" assertiveness drill in chapter two: Conquering Nervousness. It incorporates techniques from my Silat and combatives days, focusing on diffusing a potential assault before it becomes a real one.

# Books on Living Your Dreams & Excelling

### *This Year I Will*
### by M. J. Ryan

One of the best goal accomplishment books out there – the one I sent Jamey at Miracle Lake. I list it first here for a reason.

### *The 7 Habits of Highly Effective People*
### by Stephen Covey

Begin with the end in mind, insist on win-wins, spend your time doing things that are important but not urgent – these are the habits of winners. A best-selling classic for a reason. And for the family man (or woman), his *7 Habits of Highly Effective Families* is superb.

### *The Magic of Thinking Big*
### by David Schwartz

Schwartz is a master motivator, and the guy who gave me that "Action Cures Fear" insight. A favorite concept: the crippling disease of *Excusitis.* What excuses have held you back? Time to let them go.

## *Eat That Frog*
## by Brian Tracy

If you had to eat a frog, would you stretch it out for hours, nibble by nibble, or swallow it down in two quick gulps? Such is Tracy's approach to getting things done. The unpleasant stuff you have to do, knock it out first and fast, and the rest is cake. And if you don't want to read the book, there's a nice abridged audio version.

## *The One Thing*
## by Gary Keller

Achieving anything of value requires time – focused chunks of time. We must therefore prioritize that which matters most, sometimes leaving less important stuff undone. Here's how.

*Finish: Give Yourself the Gift of Done*
by Jon Acuff

Good at starting but not finishing? Join the club. Acuff explains how to conquer perfectionism and actually see your big ideas through to the end. Favorite quote: "Goals you refuse to chase don't disappear — they become ghosts that haunt you. Do you know why strangers rage at each other online [and threaten poor drummers at football games] and are so quick to be angry and offended these days? Because their passion has no other outlet."

*The Professor in the Cage:*
*Why Men Fight and Why We Like to Watch*
by Jonathan Gottschall

This one isn't so much about big goal accomplishment. But if you enjoyed *Year of the Fighter,* I think you'll enjoy *Professor in the Cage* (I sure did). Similar story, with social, historical and psychological context by an awesome writer and cool dude.

# Acknowledgements

Thanks to my wife, Lisa, for your unwavering love and support. My Year of the Fighter was in many ways your Year of the Single Mom. Thank you for taking care of the kids while I did it. And thank you, Justin, Emily and Noah, for allowing me the time, and for your unwavering support and love as well.

Thanks to Lisa, old high school buddies Mel Gonzalez, TJ Lankford and Doug Sneed, Dr. Michael Carter (the Jiu Jitsu instructor who heightened my fighting conscience) and Cousin Mike for your early reviews of and feedback on this book. "Year of the Fighter" as the title was actually Mel's idea! It's the book it is thanks to your collective input and generosity.

Thanks to #1 super fan Jill Flowers for your early and consistent encouragement. It's always nice to hear "I could see it being a bestseller" from a beta reader. Special thanks for letting me borrow your husband

"Hikemaster" Olin to recharge on treks through the Smokies.

Thanks to my editor, Debi Stansil, for your careful read, review, suggestions and coaching. To all your editor friends: I take full responsibility for made-up words and country slang. She tried her hardest to root them out.

Thanks to my mother-in-law Barbara for your impeccable "blooper snooping" (proofreading). Apologies for causing you the embarrassment of researching the proper spelling of "dammit" (she's a Baptist deacon's wife, ya'll).

Thanks to Jesse and Poke Beyers at Monroe County Boxing Club for teaching me the sweet science, as well as a thing or two about being a good man and person. I'm proud to be an alumnus of your gym, and so glad I and my kids can continue to workout there. Thanks for all you've done and are doing for our community.

Thanks to James Ogle for forgiving my carwash thievery, for sharing a small portion of your martial arts skill, and for not minding me portraying you as a small-town Chuck Norris. Our community is lucky to have you and your dojo – thank you for being a positive influence and mentor to so many – and for the open invitation to train at your gym.

Thanks to my boxing teammates and friends, Jamey, Kaiden, Triston, Orlando, Brayden, Gabriel, Gabe, Hilario, Danny, Alex, Matthew, James, Cooper, Skylar, Hannah, Ethan, son Justin and nephew Sam. Respect to all of you – respect to anyone brave enough to get in the ring and bang it out.

Thanks to my kickboxing family, Matt, Buck, Scott, Mario and Stephen. Ya'll are some tough sons of guns. Thanks for letting me be a part of that world for a while, and for getting me ready for Dalton.

Last, thanks to my official opponents in the ring: Denzel, William and Logan. As Seraph said to Neo in *Matrix Reloaded,* "You do not truly know someone until you fight them." It was a pleasure to make your acquaintance.